Exploring Identity Development and Self

Exploring Identity Development and Self

Teaching Universal Themes through Young Adult Novels

Leilya A. Pitre and Mike P. Cook

ROWMAN & LITTLEFIELD
Lanham • Boulder • New York • London

Published by Rowman & Littlefield
An imprint of The Rowman & Littlefield Publishing Group, Inc.
4501 Forbes Boulevard, Suite 200, Lanham, Maryland 20706
www.rowman.com

Copyright © 2021 by Leilya A. Pitre and Mike P. Cook

All rights reserved. No part of this book may be reproduced in any form or by any electronic or mechanical means, including information storage and retrieval systems, without written permission from the publisher, except by a reviewer who may quote passages in a review.

British Library Cataloguing in Publication Information Available

Library of Congress Cataloging-in-Publication Data

Names: Cook, Mike P., author. | Pitre, Leilya, author.
Title: Exploring identity development and self : teaching universal themes through young adult novels / Mike P. Cook and Leilya A. Pitre.
Description: Lanham, Maryland : Rowman & Littlefield, 2021. | Includes bibliographical references and index. | Summary: "This book provides classroom approaches to analysis of themes in young adult literature reflecting an array of relationships with self and the world with which adolescents engage daily. These themes include self-discovery, self-perception, differentiating between right and wrong, and making difficult choices complicated by issues of social justice"—Provided by publisher.
Identifiers: LCCN 2020048574 (print) | LCCN 2020048575 (ebook) | ISBN 9781475859829 (paperback) | ISBN 9781475859812 (cloth) | ISBN 9781475859836 (epub)
Subjects: LCSH: Young adult literature—Study and teaching (Secondary) | Young adult literature—Study and teaching (Middle school)
Classification: LCC PN59 .C646 2021 (print) | LCC PN59 (ebook) | DDC 809/.892830712—dc23
LC record available at https://lccn.loc.gov/2020048574
LC ebook record available at https://lccn.loc.gov/2020048575

Contents

Preface		vii
Acknowledgments		xi
Introduction		1
1	Adolescence, Young Adult Literature, and Thematic Explorations	5
2	From the Hero's Quest to a Journey of Self-Discovery	17
3	Conceptual Teaching Unit: Identity Exploration on the Way to Self-Discovery	29
4	Good versus Bad, Right versus Wrong, and Other Choices	51
5	Conceptual Teaching Unit: Examination of Good versus Bad, Right versus Wrong, and Other Choices	63
6	Self-Perception and Being Oneself	83
7	Conceptual Teaching Unit: Developing a Positive Self-Perception	93
Bibliography		111
Index		115
About the Authors		121

Preface

When we first began conversations about writing this book, we were immediately taken back to our own secondary ELA classrooms, students, and experiences. As teacher educators, we spend our careers preparing students to be English teachers and working with those already teaching as they seek to continue their education and development. Less often we think and act as classroom teachers ourselves, at least without having the postsecondary lens influencing our view.

This book offered us this opportunity to write and design as, and for, ELA classroom teachers and to hopefully contribute to the planning discussions teachers engage in during department meetings, during lunch duty, and over a hot cup at local coffee shops.

While we both bring different educational and cultural backgrounds and experiences to this work, we share a common desire to prepare secondary ELA teachers who guide students in meaningful, relevant, and important analysis of the texts they read and the lives they live.

After moving to the United States from Ukraine, Leilya began her career in a public middle school in Louisiana. She was well-versed in, and had appreciation for, the classics, but quickly began to understand Mark Twain's (1900) observation that "a classic is something that everybody wants to have read and nobody wants to read." In her classroom, Leilya found that students often resented their assigned canonical readings because they believed these stories to be too far removed from their own life experiences.

As a high school English teacher in a variety of geographic, sociopolitical, and educational contexts, Mike witnessed some of the same resentment Leilya noted. Throughout his career as a public school teacher, he recognized one glaring similarity across many students and contexts—the use of canonical texts and their often negative impact on student engagement and learning.

In his classroom, Mike was met with students who, at best, struggled through texts such as *Beowulf*, Shakespeare's plays, *Pride and Prejudice*, and *The Great Gatsby*. More frequently, however, Mike's students resigned themselves to not learning, as they saw little to no relevance between the texts he forced them to read and their own lived experiences.

In fact, similar to Leilya's sudden understanding of Twain's comment about the canon, Mike often felt his students were thinking what two of Don Gallo's students (2001) so eloquently stated: "A classic is a book that 'requires a teacher to figure out a glimmer of what it says'" (p. 33) and literature is "keeping in touch with the dead . . . I want to read something with a pulse" (p. 34).

It wasn't until we both made intentional decisions to select high-quality, complex Young Adult Literature (YAL) that we noticed shifts in how our students responded in class and how they engaged with the material. As a direct result of this, we have spent much of our careers examining YAL, its power in classroom instruction, and new ways of rethinking traditional literary analysis through the more relevant and recognizable characters found within the pages of YA texts.

A Note about the Canon: we recognize that the canon will continue to be used in teachers' classrooms for a variety of reasons. In many classrooms, these texts are readily accessible. In others, prescribed to semi-prescribed curricula dictate the texts to be taught, many of these representing long-taught, canonical texts. Other teachers make their own decisions to bring in the canon, whether that is toward critical canon pedagogy, to pair with YAL and multimedia texts, or any of myriad other reasons.

We also believe that canonical texts can be leveraged to, in part, address the issues and themes we discuss throughout the book, especially if teachers draw from antiracist and critical literacy approaches to interrogating and interrupting oppressive power dynamics in and around the texts students read. That is important for us to note. In this book, however, rather than simply suggesting teachers throw the canon entirely out the window (that would be a radical oversimplification), we are making a larger call for relevance to students' lives and for the power of YAL. Rather than eliminating the canon, we see more utility in knocking down the walls around the canon and creating room for many other complex texts of literary merit and then allowing teachers the autonomy to make their own decisions around what and how students read.

There are, of course, as many teachers who are not only interested in bringing more YAL into their classrooms as there are teachers also unsure how to secure the funding necessary to purchase large numbers of books. While there is no easy answer to this, we have found a few avenues to be fruitful. Teachers, for example, can draw on the power of social media (e.g., the collective wisdom at @ncte and #ncte) for direction and ideas. We also believe taking time to speak with media center coordinators and administrators can be time well spent. There are often funds in schools for book purchases, but those funds are not always advertised widely to teachers.

There are also small grants, such as those offered by local entities, worth pursuing. Mike, for example, secured two small grants from his local energy consortium for purchasing books for his high school classroom library. We have also seen a great number of teachers going grassroots and starting go-fund-me-style fundraisers to help support the cause. Our point: while we wish all teachers had access to ample funding for books, we simply know this isn't the case across the country, and we want to encourage them to tug at any/every funding thread available.

Our goal in these pages is to create space for conversations around thematic inquiry, especially regarding the ways students are or are not engaged by and connected to many of the traditional texts they encounter. In short, we hope to offer teachers new ways to look at, and new texts for studying, a few literary themes that have persisted in classroom instruction for decades.

We hope you find assistance in these pages. Happy reading.

Leilya A. Pitre and Mike P. Cook

Acknowledgments

I would like to thank my husband and daughters for their continuous support, patience, and listening. Without a strong and safe home front, it would be difficult to devote so much time to work and writing. Next, my sincere gratitude goes to all of my teachers. You didn't just teach me reading, writing, and following grammar rules; you encouraged me to think and face challenges without running away in difficult situations. Thank you to my students, former and current. You are my most rewarding audience, and you are the ones who implement everything—well, mostly everything—I create in my head and plan for you to accomplish in my classroom. Finally, thank you, Mike. You are an incredible person and a great writing partner, and collaboration with you has taught me to see this work as gradual progress and growth toward the final result.
—Leilya

Thank you to my family, Sara and Sawyer, for providing me time and space to write, breaks from writing (excuses to avoid writing?), and the support and motivation to push on. When I think about when this book was written, during the 2020 COVID-19 pandemic, I am reminded of just how indebted I am to you two. My appreciation is beyond words. Leilya, thank you for inviting me to join this project, your brainchild. I hope I've been helpful. We've definitely balanced one another out nicely, and I'm reminded regularly of the benefits of collaboration. Thank you also to all the teachers and educators out there drawing on the power of YAL in their instruction and to those who continue to sing its many praises. You are appreciated.
—Mike

We also would like to thank Brandon Sams, Sharon Kane, Paula Greathouse, and Steven Bickmore, our generous colleagues, who read the manuscript and provided helpful feedback. Thank you finally to the Rowman & Littlefield publishing editors, Carlie Wall and Tom Koerner, for guidance in preparing this book for submission and publishing.

Introduction

As children grow up, they experience various life events involving a wide spectrum of human relationships with people, nature and the world around them, including love, friendship, loyalty, betrayal, hate, death, loss, hope, and many more. Each encounter and each experience cause certain reactions, followed by reflection, and the lessons learned from any given situation inform their choices and decisions later. To help children understand their experiences as well as what is happening around them, English teachers use literature and literary characters who undergo similar experiences and learn crucial life lessons or insights about life and the world around us.

These lessons are what we call themes in literature. Many of these themes are universal because they may be applied to anyone regardless of cultural differences or geographic location. However, each of the universal themes found in literature has a specific message to readers, and this message is individual, contextual, and ever-changing.

One thing that has not changed much over the years is the English class reading curriculum. Books that are required for middle and high school students still heavily rely on literary canon. For decades, English teachers throughout the country have used many of the same literary titles to examine universal themes and the lessons they carry. Traditionally, to discuss first love, teachers turn to Shakespeare's *Romeo and Juliet*. To draw attention to topics around bravery, courage, and/or the archetypal hero, *Beowulf* or *The Odyssey* are the classic texts taught. *The Great Gatsby* is regularly employed to explore the concept of the American Dream. The durability of the canon is impressive; however, it signals the often limited outlook on the secondary school reading choices.

As much as the lessons learned from canonic texts can be applicable to many students, and schools have long held to these lists as necessary texts for the study of literature, history, and culture, many of these texts are outdated and do not resonate with adolescents and their lives and experiences today. The development of society, increasing diversity in classrooms, and changing times lead to different experiences, and what worked to resolve conflicts in the past may not be effective, or even useful, for the diverse student population in twenty-first-century classrooms.

Teenagers these days live in a different world, a world made up of myriad cultures, beliefs, and ways of being; they are facing different problems, in different contexts, and their existences are complicated by advanced technological progress in a time when much communication occurs across space and time with a click of a button on a favorite electronic device. Despite the enormous progress, they experience the struggles of identity crisis, first love and heartbreak, face the pain of a friend's betrayal, or deal with the death of a loved one, just like countless generations of adolescents before them. These young people need to see they are not the only ones going through adolescent life trials and tribulations.

Young adults need new books and new characters in which they are able to see themselves. Thankfully, a rapid growth of Young Adult Literature (YAL) allows us to choose appropriate texts of high quality to use in the classroom. This book offers middle and high school teachers, as well as teacher educators working with preservice teachers, ways to explore universal literary themes through YA texts and by creating spaces for frank, relevant, engaging, and meaningful conversations with adolescent readers.

The book is organized by chapters. Chapter 1 serves as an initial building block connecting adolescence, YAL, and foundations of a thematic analysis. It begins with defining adolescence as a complex and unique period of growth and development of young people. The chapter reminds teachers about the importance of knowing students in the classroom, their reading preferences, and how to engage them in reading resulting in critical thinking. Further, we discuss YAL as a literary category, its characteristics, and its possibilities in the classroom. The chapter concludes with helpful approaches to teaching thematic explorations.

The following six chapters of the book are organized by themes. Chapters 2, 3, and 6 serve as thematic chapters, and each introduces one of the universal themes and explores its messages using a representative young adult novel. Chapters 3, 5, and 7 offer instructional units and are paired with the corresponding thematic chapter.

The first thematic chapter, chapter 2 invites readers to reimagine a traditional universal theme of a hero's quest into a journey of self-discovery helping students at the middle and high school levels to think about themselves, their place, and identity. The authors discuss a traditional approach to teaching the hero's quest and suggest alternative ways to build thematic investigations that will be relevant and accessible to students in the classroom. A suggested YA novel for the first theme examination is Matt de la Peña's *Mexican Whiteboy* (2008).

Following thematic analysis of the previous chapter, chapter 3 presents an instructional teaching unit using de la Peña's novel to foster literary study around the journey of self-discovery and, as a result, an exploration into students' own identities. This chapter provides teachers with a possible outline of the unit with activities and assessments that allow students to think critically about identity and its development, draw connections between literary characters and their personal lives, and attempt to analyze their place in the classroom, neighborhood community, and/or society as a whole. As a result, the unit allows students to develop and apply the academic skill of thematic analysis and adds to their personal growth and self-construction.

The next chapter focuses on the universal theme of Good versus Bad, Right versus Wrong, and making difficult choices. It builds a thematic context via short stories, fairy tales, myths, legends, and later Shakespearean plays. Chapter 4 argues that adolescents today live in a different reality, and what was considered good centuries ago may not be valued as such today, that is, the concepts of right and wrong might also shift. *All American Boys* (2015), a YA novel by Jason Reynolds and Brendan Kiely, is used to analyze the theme and its implications for young people making tough decisions in a twenty-first-century society.

To assist teachers with planning, chapter 5 showcases an instructional unit with *All American Boys* as an anchor text. The thematic explorations of good or bad and right or wrong are complicated by the difficult choices the protagonists have to make in response to police brutality and racial profiling. This unit allows students and teachers to grapple with anti-racism in a safe classroom environment by participating in activities and projects that gradually prepare them for challenging conversations. Along with the thematic analysis, the unit engages students to develop advanced argumentative writing skills supported by research.

The third theme of this volume—self-perception and being oneself—is established in chapter 6. It cogitates adolescents' paths to developing a positive self-perception and logically continues the themes of self-discovery (chapter 2) and making the right choices (chapter 4). The authors believe that studying self-perception leads students to self-acceptance complemented by self-construction and finding points of belonging in the world. The graphic novel *American Born Chinese* (Yang, 2006) fuels thematic investigations of this chapter.

Finally, chapter 7 concludes the book with a teaching unit created as an example to study the theme of self-perception and being oneself. In addition to *American Born Chinese,* this unit includes Marjane Satrapi's graphic memoir *Persepolis* (2003) as the second anchor text. The suggested examples of activities and assessments continue enhancing students' academic skills in reading, writing, speaking, and language use, and require them to use textual analysis to connect texts to their own lives, and as a lens for viewing self-worth and self-growth.

For each of the themes, we propose a YA text at the core of explorations. Needless to say, this is just a suggestion. Teachers may use a different novel, combination of texts, and/or use a variety of supplemental readings. Each of the instructional chapters provides a list of multimodal supplemental texts that can be used within the proposed unit and additional resources for teachers and educators, including other YA fiction titles with diverse young men and women characters, representatives of different cultural, ethnic, and socio-economic backgrounds, as well as those who identify as LGBTQ. There are also nonfiction texts, media, and web resources.

Undeniably, there are many more books that can address the universal themes discussed in this book. We encourage teachers and educators to read this textbook and note our novel selections as simply examples. It is up to instructors how they may use the presented instructional units; they may, for example, be applied in their entirety or modified for a specific grade level or classroom. The same goes for the activities; they can smoothly transition with necessary adaptations to fit specific teaching objectives and students' needs. Our goal is to assist with developing rich learning experiences and to provide teachers with initial ideas, approaches, and resources.

Chapter 1

Adolescence, Young Adult Literature, and Thematic Explorations

ADOLESCENCE AND ADOLESCENT READERS

Defining Adolescence

Attempting to agree on a precise definition of adolescence has been and continues to be a source of debate. With each generation, adolescence and the field's understanding of it shifts and changes. As a result, there have been inconsistencies and disagreement in attempts to singularly define and place age parameters around adolescence as a construct and phase of life.

Sometimes adolescence is defined in years of age (e.g., ten to eighteen, twelve to eighteen, and even as much as a twenty-six-year span). Other times, it is defined as the period of time spanning the beginning of puberty and an establishment of independence. While perhaps more of an oversimplification, adolescence is often described as the transition from childhood to adulthood and is often separated into three categories or stages: early adolescence, middle adolescence, and late adolescence.

Adolescents, as part of this time of development, experience an increase in pressure (in relation to those around them), in decision making, and in a search for self or an attempt to establish their own priorities and norms. This period of time is viewed as complex and multifactored and encompasses the movement from being seen as reliant and dependent to being seen as having agency, accountability, and independence.

Adolescence is a unique time in a young person's life and in their growth and development, and it includes the development of the physical body, behavior, relationships, cognition, emotion, and so forth, as well as changes in relationships with friends, family, and self. It is also useful to note, especially in a book about universal themes in literature, that in many societies, "adolescence" is not considered or recognized as a formal stage of development. Even in the United States and other industrialized nations, it wasn't until after the late 1800s that the concept of adolescence began to develop and be considered. As a result of the inconsistencies, across the board it becomes even more important for teachers to know their students. For the purposes of this book, however, we consider adolescents to be secondary (grades 6–12) school-aged students.

Teaching Adolescents

Perhaps first, teachers must remember that teens today, as Bucher and Hinton (2014) argue, often develop—physically, cognitively, and socially—earlier and more quickly than in previous generations, and they face a variety of issues and challenges that may not have been as prevalent previously. Educators must also be aware of, and draw on, the diversity within the classroom and adolescents as individuals, as development is not a singular, universal pathway (Manning & Bucher, 2009).

Likewise, teachers should make an effort to get to know their students and their unique lives, experiences, and challenges. It is important to avoid generalizing the "typical" adolescent and to acknowledge that they enter classrooms from many places, some more privileged than others in their ability to safely navigate the adolescent years.

Just as adolescents are diverse with regard to how they identify, what they like and don't like, and how they exist in the world, so too are they coming to classrooms from a variety of cultures, beliefs, and homes. Some students, for example, are expected to be more adult-like, by caring for siblings and family members, working to support families, and so on in their outside-of-school lives. Others have experienced challenges and hardships that unfortunately include the loss of loved ones, poverty, homelessness, living independently, war, the loss of childhood and adolescence, and uncertainty that their classmates, and even their teachers, have not. Others still struggle to find relevance and to see pieces of themselves in the work they are asked to do at school.

As a result, and to design instruction that can foster self-assessment in students and that can provide them opportunities to truly learn more about themselves and to grow as humans, teachers must remember that adolescence is not a static concept, but is instead experienced by students across a spectrum. Stated another way, all instructional design for adolescents, including that described throughout this book, should begin with the individual teacher's knowledge of their students.

With this in mind, it is also vital that classroom teachers create safe and supportive spaces for students to embark on the complicated journeys of finding themselves. Such a space can begin with attention to the classroom environment, one that includes relationship building (student/student and student/teacher), collaboration and interaction with peers, and supportive teachers who view them as complex and capable.

Yet another part of working with adolescents has to do with relevancy and scaffolding. Helping adolescents make sense of their lives and the world includes making learning relevant. Relevant instruction, in part, involves providing a balance of support/scaffolding and independence so that students have structured freedom to learn and make meaning in their own ways and in their own lives. In short, teachers should focus on engagement and motivation, both byproducts of relevance. Finally, one way to support students, and a necessary step toward student independence, is through intentional modeling of the types of thinking, reading, being, and learning in which teachers want their students to engage.

Adolescents and Reading

Going beyond what teachers should know when working with adolescents, it is equally helpful to consider adolescents themselves, in this case what and how they read. The reading habits of adolescents are influenced by a number of diverse factors (e.g., community, development, and experiences). Thus, the reasons adolescents read and the texts they choose to read are just as diverse (Bucher & Hinton, 2014).

Adolescent readers want to and need to, through literature, interrogate life and all that it includes, and they look for characters who look like them and who experience similar problems and situations that parallel their lives (Bean & Rigoni, 2001), which Bean and Moni (2003) suggest are provided by Young Adult Literature (YAL). This kind of literature becomes their ally in learning, personal development, and growth.

The literature adolescents read serves, in many ways, as backgrounds of experience, where they use fictional characters, settings, and experiences to reflect on (and to compare to) their own lives and to foster development—in much the same way they do during real world interactions and experiences. It is precisely for this reason that YAL has become so popular with adolescent readers—as Stallworth (2006) suggests, YAL is an "electrifying genre for getting today's young adolescents reading and exploring who they are" (p. 59).

Adolescents and Critical Reading

One way to support adolescent readers in engaging in the type of literary analysis and personal growth described in this book is to foster critical skills in them—that is, the skills that allow them to make personal connections to texts and to critically analyze and reflect on the books they read. This begins with thoughtful text selection and instructional design, examples of which can be found in subsequent chapters.

Related to text selection, teachers should also make critical discussion and the use of critical lenses central to all literature instruction in the classroom. Teachers can (and should) create time and space for students to make personal connections to the literature they read. Students require the opportunity to try out, practice, and to ultimately take up these lenses and skills and to learn the reflective habits of mind necessary for deep and meaningful literary analysis.

Finally, teachers should do exactly what good teachers do—continue to be learners and listeners. There are myriad resources, from amazing teachers and scholars, available for consideration. This text serves as only one resource, so teachers should go further and borrow from frameworks such as Bean and Moni's (2003) adaptation of Morgan's (1998) critical discussion prompts and Thein et al.'s (2011) Critical Literature Circles as they design instruction meant to foster critical thinking and meaningful development in students.

This book provides teachers and educators with suggestions for using complex, high-quality YAL to create learning opportunities for students that will draw their attention to literature and promote further critical thinking and reflection. The section below illustrates characteristics and possibilities of YAL that place it in this advantageous position in the English classroom.

YAL AND ITS POSSIBILITIES IN THE CLASSROOM

YAL and Its Characteristics

While some readers and experts call it adolescent literature and others prefer teen or juvenile literature, this book will use the term *young adult literature* without delving into stylistic and semantic differences among the other terms. Another important note to make is to acknowledge that YAL is a literary category, not a genre, and, as such, it includes the works of all the literary genres (i.e., prose, drama, and poetry), their subgenres (e.g., historic, realistic, or dystopian fiction, verse novels, sci-fi, fantasy, mystery, nonfiction narratives), and multimodal representations (e.g., graphic novels, podcasts, and audiobooks).

Since YAL is a relatively new literary category, teachers, librarians, literary critics, educators, and even publishers have not yet come to an agreement about the exact definition of YAL (Aronson, 2002). Among dozens of definitions of YAL (see, e.g., Aronson, 2001; Bucher & Hinton, 2010; Bushman &

Bushman, 1997; Cart, 2008; Herz & Gallo, 2005), there are a few that reflect what this literature represents and its intended audience.

Many of the literary experts favor Donelson and Nilsen's (1997) functional definition of YA literature as anything a young adult will "choose to read" (p. 6) as a reminder that teachers should not limit their students' choices (Kaywell, 2001). However, this definition does not offer much explanation of the term as it does not clarify the kind of literature young people may choose. They may select to read Danielle Steele, Steven King, John Grisham, or Kate Chopin; however, these authors' works may hardly be considered young adult texts.

Other literary scholars consider YAL as what is marketed for young adults. This is also problematic because young adults may not read what is marketed for them, or what is marketed for them may not be written with them in mind. There are also definitions that point to the age of adolescent readers, marking it somewhere between ten and twenty years old. For example, Hayn and Bach (2011) point out that YAL works are "those texts written for audiences between the ages of 12 and 18" (p.173). A more sufficient definition for this book would be the one formulated by Herz and Gallo (2005), which encapsulates the main characteristics of YAL.

Herz and Gallo define YAL as texts in which teenagers are the main characters dealing with issues to which young adults can relate, consequences are mostly determined by the choices and decisions of main characters, and "all traditional literary elements typical of classical literature" can be identified in these stories (2005, pp. 10–11). To develop an even bigger picture definition, Bucher and Hinton (2010) compile the most distinct characteristics of YAL using several scholarly sources:

> Young adult literature will be defined as literature in prose and verse that has excellence of form or expression in its genre (Merriam-Webster's Encyclopedia of Literature, 1995), provides a unique adolescent point of view (Hertz & Gallo, 1996), and reflects the concerns, interests, and challenges of contemporary young adults (Brown & Stephens, 1995). In sum, it provides a roadmap for readers 12 to 20 years of age (Bean & Moni, 2003, p. 8).

This definition encompasses the notion that YAL is written with adolescent readers in mind and addresses their interactions with the world, in which protagonists are young adults telling their stories. It also establishes YAL as relevant to teenagers and different from many canonical texts not written specifically for adolescents (Glaus, 2014).

The roots of YAL were planted in 1942, when Maureen Daly released her *Seventeenth Summer* for publication. It was the first book considered to be targeting teenagers as the reading audience, according to Michael Cart

(2008), an author and the former president of the Young Adult Library Services Association. The term "young adult," representing the twelve to eighteen age range of readers, was devised by the Young Adult Library Services Association during the 1960s. Initially, Cart points out, YAL "referred to realistic fiction that was set in the real (as opposed to imagined), contemporary world and addressed problems, issues, and life circumstances of interest to young readers aged approximately 12–18" (2008, para. 2).

Following Daly's novel, published YAL novels—S.E. Hinton's *The Outsiders* (1967), and Robert Lipsyte's *The Contender* (1967), among the works of Judy Blume, Lois Duncan, and Robert Cormier—offered mature realistic fiction with themes and social issues relevant to adolescents. Since then, the body of literary work attributed to this category has grown exponentially. Today's YA texts represent a wide range of styles, genres and subgenres, and modalities and forms.

YAL is "as varied as the multimedia mix of teenagers' lives, as complex as their stormy emotional landscapes, as profound as their soul-shaping searches for identity, as vital as their nation-forming future" (Aronson, 2001, p. 11). It caters to diverse readers from different cultural, ethnic, and racial backgrounds, to adolescents living in rural or urban communities, those who are privileged or marginalized based on any of the aforementioned characteristics or belong to LGBTQ groups, representing lower, middle, or upper social class or anything in between.

Moreover, these works are written by diverse writers responding to the We Need Diverse Books organization whose mission is to put "more books featuring diverse characters into the hands of all children" (see https://diversebooks.org/). The goal of this organization is to support production and promotion of literature that reflects and honors the lives of all young people. The organization's website provides a variety of resources and recommendations for young adult readers, teachers, and librarians.

YAL as Complex and Rigorous

Since the beginning of the YAL field in 1960–1970s, young adult texts and young adult readers have changed drastically. Books are speaking "directly to teens themselves, not teachers or librarians," notices Campbell (2004, p. 63), and the authors incorporate more complex characters, subjects, and situations (Cart, 2001), introducing various forms and narration patterns. YAL today quickly responds to societal progress and problems, reflecting technology advances and multimodality of information sources, as well as topics of social injustice, cruelty, bullying, mental health issues, and many more.

Literary scholars believe that today's YAL is of high quality; it is "sophisticated, complex, and powerful" (Stallworth, 2006, p. 59). However, to appeal to young adults and to be worthy of reading and studying, YAL should satisfy three major criteria, as outlined by Bucher and Hinton:

- It should reflect young adults' age and development by addressing their reading abilities, thinking levels, and interest levels.
- It should deal with contemporary issues, problems, and experiences with characters to whom adolescents can relate.
- It should consider contemporary world perspectives, including cultural, social, and gender diversity; environmental issues; global politics; and international interdependence (pp. 9–10).

Despite a wide variety of forms and narrative tools employed, YAL has many common characteristics:

1. Unique voice and narration. The story is usually told in the first-person point of view of a protagonist(s) or from the third person point of view, which is limited and very close to the protagonist(s). This way, readers still have a feeling that it is narrated through the main character's eyes.
2. The main character is a teenager who is the center of the plot. A number of recent YA novels have two or more protagonists/narrators at the center of the plot, including *He Said, She Said* (Alexander, 2013), *All American Boys* (Reynolds & Kiely, 2015), and *I Have Lost My Way* (Forman, 2018).
3. The story is happening in teen years, not about the teen years.
4. Conflicts are consistent with young adult experiences, so themes are of interest to young people.
5. Adults are often missing or only play a minor role, and their perspective is limited.
6. The language is very accessible and reflects the language of adolescents.
7. The plot is concise with a more limited time span, often around two to three months and less frequently up to a year in the characters' lives.

There are more characteristics of YAL, but these are the ones that help make YAL appealing to adolescent readers.

Possibilities of YAL in the English Classroom

To say that adolescents are attracted to YAL is not surprising. One of the pioneer advocates for the use of YAL in the classrooms, Gary Salvner explained that young adult texts are "about adolescents and for adolescents" (2000, p. 96) as they center learning around students. These literary texts "illustrate for young people what literature can be, moving them and revealing to them how literature builds knowledge" (p. 97), which is ultimately a major goal of English teachers and of the English classroom.

If YAL makes adolescents think, reflect, and build knowledge, it is worth introducing it into the classroom. Educators who believe that age-appropriate literature is one of the major criteria for choosing YAL as a teaching tool and content argue that these works are more suitable for middle and high school students. To create engaged reading and learning experiences, students need to see how and where the texts they read and their own lives intersect. It is from this intersection that many supporters of YAL promote these texts' potential to support a life-long love of reading while addressing issues vital to their development (Glaus, 2014).

YAL scholars believe that the breadth and depth of YAL are of high quality and that the universal themes of love, death, loss, racism, and friendship, which educators value so much in the canonical literature, are also present in young adult texts. Due to realistic settings and believable characters speaking the language of adolescents, YA novels make complex and pressing societal and personal issues concrete and understandable for contemporary students.

One of the most beneficial outcomes of using YAL in the classroom is the ability of these texts to bridge the differences and make vital connections between the "big" world, school, neighborhood community, and students' personal life struggles and challenges and help students feel less invisible, ignored, or marginalized. It also gives them voice and actively engages them in discussions of the difficult and sensitive problems within society, thus preparing them for adulthood and change.

To summarize the favorable possibilities of YAL in the classroom, it is necessary to mention that YA texts provide:

- a vast selection of high-quality texts at various reading levels;
- opportunities for enhancement of reading, writing, speaking, and listening skills;
- complex text for students to analyze, interpret, and evaluate;
- enjoyable reading experiences;
- prospects for cross-curricular studies;
- connections to alienated students;
- "windows" and "mirrors" for students' lives;
- possibilities for discussions to address important issues in students' lives and in the world around them, including their identity search and issues of self-acceptance, self-worth, and self-construction.

These and many other accompanying possibilities of YAL earn this literary category a valued and rightful position in secondary language arts classrooms.

Noticing the enthusiastic response of adolescents and their teachers to YA texts of various genres, publishing houses around the country work with educators to prepare and publish textbooks to help teachers effectively use new literature in the classrooms. Roman & Littlefield, for example, have over thirty titles, across a range of topics, approaches, and fields, dedicated to YAL. Some of their recent powerful texts discussing YAL in education include:

- *Breaking the Taboo with Young Adult Literature*, by Victor Malo-Juvera and Paula Greathouse (2020)
- *Reading for Action: Engaging Youth in Social Justice through Young Adult Literature*, by Ashley S. Boyd and Janine J. Darragh (2019)
- *Representing the Rainbow in Young Adult Literature: LGBTQ+ Content since 1969*, by Christine A. Jenkins and Michael Cart (2018)
- *Teaching Young Adult Literature Today: Insights, Considerations, and Perspectives for the Classroom Teacher*, edited by Judith A. Hayn and Jeffrey S. Kaplan (2016)
- *Young Adult Literature and the Digital World: Textual Engagement through Visual Literacy*, edited by Jennifer S. Dail, Shelbie Witte, and Steven T. Bickmore (2018).

TEACHING THEME ANALYSIS

Themes are abstract ideas, and teaching them can be challenging because it often leaves students confused or frustrated. Frankly, many teachers often struggle to teach theme analysis, including finding ways to explain and walk students through the analytic process. Before attempting to analyze a theme of the story or novel, students have to clearly distinguish among the following terms: main idea, topic, and theme. Too often these are used interchangeably, which can create more confusion. Here is a brief reminder.

The *main idea* generally tells us what the story is about and can be formulated in a brief, one-sentence summary. For example, the main idea of *Lion King* may be formulated as follows: A young lion grows strength and courage to defeat his evil uncle and is able to reclaim his kingdom.

The *topic* is an important subject, usually one word that is presented or revealed within the story. There are at least two obvious topics in *Lion King*: responsibility and courage. Topics, much like universal themes, just name the main subject(s) of stories.

The *theme* is a statement that a story is making about the main subject or topic. It is an insight about human life that is conveyed in the literary work. What do we learn about responsibility from *Lion King*? It may be expressed in this statement: Everyone has to grow up and assume responsibilities, leaving childhood behind at some point.

Practicing how to differentiate and identify main ideas, topics, and themes consistently is a key for building up skills of literary analysis. One great way to do that is to begin with short stories with which most of the students in the classroom are familiar. Fairy tales, such as *Cinderella*, *Red Riding Hood*, or *The Wolf and the Seven Lambs* can be a starting point. Teachers may use an easy graphic organizer simply dividing the page into three columns placing the words "main idea," "topic," and "theme" on top of each column. To help even more, the brief definitions can be included under each term.

When people read books, they enter into a conversation with the author about what matters about life, society, human behavior, and so on (Smith & Wilhelm, 2010). At the core of this imaginable exchange is comprehension. To effectively explore a theme of the story, students have to have a firm grip on setting, characters, and plot. These elements determine and project a path of the theme development in the story.

Identifying a theme is a great skill, but it is not enough. Teachers have to go beyond recognizing themes and teach students how to analyze themes and their development in a literary work. Similar to differentiating among topics, ideas, and themes, this work should be gradual and consistent. Themes are not just the lessons for the characters in the story; they are also lessons intended by the author for readers.

Thematic explorations are complicated by the fact that themes are subjective and might be interpreted differently by readers. That is, two students analyzing the theme with a main topic of courage, for example, may come to statements that differ based on their individual understanding. Teachers should explain that it is acceptable and happens in real life as well. People are different, and they have various understandings of the same issues.

Teachers may organize the preparation for discussion of a novel's themes in small group and whole-class activities. They may begin with exercises that strengthen comprehension of the text and prepare for thematic analysis. Students may be tasked with identifying settings and their significance, finding or categorizing plot events, creating cause and effect charts to trace the characters' reactions to events, and differentiating between main ideas and topics, as discussed earlier.

These purposeful activities create a basis for theme identification and analysis. Based on the main topics, teachers may offer story-specific questions that will lead to formulating themes. For example, if students detect courage as the main topic of the story, teachers may ask them to answer these questions keeping in mind the topic of courage and supporting it with concrete textual evidence:

- What is the major event in the story and how did it happen?
- How did the characters react to this event?
- What important decisions did the characters make?
- How did the characters grow and change in the novel?
- What did the characters learn?
- What can I learn from their experience?

To guide the purposeful thematic analysis, teachers may add questions to include the settings or language and its use and how these elements are significant in understanding the main topic. However, the final two questions should always remain.

These last two questions are asking about the theme of the story, but do so in a clear and specific way. Unlike the intimidating and too general question students are so used to hearing in the classroom ("What is the theme of this story?"), students are able to connect the plot events, characters' reactions, decisions, and consequences of these decisions. Thus formulating the theme becomes a logical, concluding step because what they do answering these questions is actually the theme analysis.

At this point, if students are tasked with a theme analysis essay, they may begin with a formulated theme as a strong thesis in the introduction and throughout the paper demonstrate how the plot, characters, settings, and/or language devices support this theme throughout the story. An additional lesson or two may be devoted to gathering and properly using the textual support.

To assist teachers and educators in organizing theme analysis and thoughtful discussions, the following chapters of this volume offer helpful materials. Chapters 2 (self-discovery), 4 (making difficult choices), and 6 (developing positive self-perception) provide thematic explorations around novels chosen as anchor texts for thematic inquiry units of instruction. Chapters 3, 5, and 7 demonstrate how teachers may approach these thematic units by providing activities and tasks leading to effective and meaningful theme examination.

Chapter 2

From the Hero's Quest to a Journey of Self-Discovery

THEMATIC CONTEXT AND TRADITIONAL APPROACHES

As part of adolescence, teenagers are trying to figure out who they are and how they fit into their immediate surroundings to make more sense of the world in which they live. This becomes even more complicated when these adolescents move from a familiar middle school setting to a new high school. Young, vulnerable people find themselves in a foreign environment with strangers, whether they are peers or teachers.

While their peers are often in the same shoes, teachers are in a position to help and guide students through these challenging times. However, often, they begin a new school year by offering the first literary unit on a "hero's journey," a journey that is most likely far removed from their students' lives and daily experiences.

Traditionally, a unit on the hero's journey revolves around reading texts, such as *The Odyssey*, an ancient Greek epic poem attributed to Homer. Planning the unit, teachers claim that by studying the hero's journey and the associated archetypes, "students gain a better understanding of storytelling patterns, examine their personal concept of a hero, and learn how heroes are a universal theme in literature" (Hamby, 2018). This knowledge is valuable without a doubt; however, there are several drawbacks to such an approach.

These learning objectives fail to connect to students' lives, especially when grounded in Campbell's definition of a hero: "A hero is someone who has given his or her life to something bigger than oneself" (2008). Such a realization creates opportunity and space for teachers to adapt traditional instructional and thematic approaches to students' study of the hero by viewing it through a plural, contextual lens instead of the oft-used singular view.

Often the unit on the hero's journey is based on the seminal work of Joseph Campbell (2008), an inspiring teacher, lecturer, researcher, and author of several books exploring the mythology and the archetypal hero carrying similar features across diverse cultures. A lifetime of research allowed Campbell to identify many common patterns occurring in hero myths and stories from around the world.

Campbell synthesized his findings, outlining several basic stages that almost every hero-quest undertakes regardless of the culture it belongs to. Campbell calls this common structure "the monomyth." Based on this monomyth, the hero's journey is usually taught as a three-part endeavor, one in which the hero progresses through three major acts:

1. The Departure Act is the beginning of the journey, when the hero accepts the challenge, commits to an expedition, and leaves the Ordinary World.
2. The Initiation Act: the hero travels into an unknown land, that is, the "Special World" and is transforming into a true leader by conquering fear, facing danger and even a downfall, and securing victory.
3. The Return Act: the hero returns triumphant into the Ordinary World. The hero survives death, overcomes his greatest fear, slays the dragon, and earns some kind of a reward.

Throughout such a unit, students explore the essential qualities of a leader and/or hero, as articulated in the epic, and the journey requires a person undertaking it to become a hero. While Campbell's monomyth perfectly reflects the traditional forms of a quest—folk and fairy tales, myths, and legends—it can also be connected to students' individual lives and the world and communities they inhabit. A quest does not have to include an underground kingdom, monsters, magic forces, swords, or "the elixir." This quest can be taught and interpreted as a real-life journey, which every single person undertakes in order to grow and change.

Analyzing universally accepted characteristics of epic heroes, teachers frequently emphasize that many of their qualities—bravery, honesty, dignity, selflessness, kindness, and so on—are still valued, as they are the indicators of a strong personality able to make difficult choices and face life challenges. This is an important and much-needed lesson; however, it is also crucial that adolescents recognize that each one of them may discover and develop these qualities on their own terms, considering their experiences.

As we noted above, many of the traditional approaches to teaching the hero's journey (often through texts like *The Odyssey*, *Beowulf*, and *The Iliad*) fail to connect to all students, their lives, and their experiences. These texts are traditionally focused on pain, trouble, and difficulty, which can suggest to learners that negative connotations, and often outcomes, accompany the concept of the hero, impacting how students define heroes in relation to their own identities and experiences.

Studying a text, such as *The Odyssey*, asks students to compare themselves to Odysseus and his experiences, which immediately suggests similarity rather than acknowledging plurality and valuing differences. In many ways, it also suggests that everyone should become a hero, a leader, and someone who becomes larger than their current life. Such an expectation is unrealistic and burdensome and may contribute additional pressures to their lives, which are already complicated in many unique ways.

Traditional hero narratives often tend to be very male and masculine focused and position women in supplementary and problematic roles. Such texts create over-masculinized narratives and suggest that heroes look and act one way, severely limiting the number of students who can see pieces of themselves in these characters. As part of a literary study of the hero and of engaging students in journeys of self-discovery and self-construction, it is vital we make intentional efforts to expand the ways heroes are represented in traditional literature and in our classrooms.

Part of these intentional efforts involves introducing students to diversity in sexual representation and gender diversity in heroes, those who identify, for example, as LGBTQ, as girls and women, and as other nontraditional representations of heroes. Such an approach begins to recognize the myriad contributions of female, queer, and racially and ethnically diverse heroes in the world and in texts.

Additionally, it is worth discussing with students that not everyone strives to be a leader, a recognized hero, or a savior of people. In other words, striving to be a visible and vocal contributor is not a necessary prerequisite to heroism. It is also quite possible to be individuals who do great little things and do those things quietly, anonymously, and/or in supportive roles.

Similarly, the hero narrative is commonly taught as something to aspire to, asking students to view each of these characters as lofty and worthy of their praise. To teach the hero in this way misses important opportunities for students to complicate the decisions the hero makes, the ways he creates his own difficulties, his questionable moral and ethical character, and so forth.

The texts we have historically taught around the hero and toward the purposes of self-discovery, upon close and critical reads, fail to represent and engage our students in a variety of ways. First, texts such as *The Odyssey* fail to consider relevancy for our students. The text itself is ancient, foreign, and dense. The language is often difficult to read, and several of these texts are epic poems written in verse, adding yet another layer of complication for contemporary students.

Second, these traditional texts and approaches often suggest that everything works out in the hero's favor in the end. In other words, the hero always wins. Such an optimistic view doesn't account for the complexity of students' lived experiences, their hopes and dreams, their wins and losses. One potentially problematic message in this approach is that a clear path to success, change, or transformation must be present in order for one to take the journey.

Third, the ways we have long taught the hero's journey fail to acknowledge variations in the journey. For example, texts, such as *The Odyssey*, fall short of valuing or even representing journey stories of immigration, displacement, struggle with sexuality, and so on. The traditional journey simply does not take into account the myriad experiences humans have and that heroes do not have. Moreover, the traditional journey narrative and the ways we teach it fail to acknowledge that heroes can develop, that is, they can change and evolve, and their journeys can develop and branch out in different directions.

With this thought of continuous development, teachers may actively engage students in exploring the concept of self-construction. Understanding that there is not a self already defined, waiting to be found, students might be relieved and encouraged to "construct" their future self. They have control over the kind of self they choose, striving to change to be their best selves.

One need not look further than contemporary superhero comics and films for relevant and powerful examples of heroes that embark on a range of journeys, some with positive outcomes and some with negative. These characters expand our traditional understandings of the hero, for example, with regard to age, gender, sexuality, race, and so forth, and, as a result, may connect with a more diverse readership.

Perhaps, it is time we rethink which heroes deserve our time, which more fully connect to the lives of our students, and which no longer do the job. And relatedly, perhaps, it is time we rethink the texts and hero narratives we bring into our classrooms and the ways we foster opportunities for students to engage in their own journeys of self-discovery. That is, efforts to engage in culturally relevant and sustaining pedagogical practices require teachers to know their students and to use that knowledge to rethink texts commonly used in classrooms and the related thematic study asked of students.

DRAWING CONNECTIONS TO STUDENTS' LIVES

While valuing the study of myths, legends, and folktales as educative and enriching the background knowledge about archetypal heroes, anti-heroes, their characteristics, and roles in literature, teachers have to consider ways to connect this knowledge and literary experiences to students' lives. As noted previously in this chapter, this begins by teachers taking the time to truly get to know their students, including their experiences, cultures, beliefs, languages, funds of knowledge, and other individual values they bring with them into classrooms.

To this end, teachers may pose important reflective questions to themselves, such as: How is it possible to draw connections between the hero's journey and the journey of self-discovery we want students to undertake? What are the points of intersection? What are the points of divergence? Most importantly, what do the answers to those two questions mean for teaching and learning in the ELA classroom? As teachers, how might we create meaningful and relevant learning experiences, rather than those that students believe to be detached and irrelevant to their lives, for students? That is, how can we design instruction around the journey of self-discovery in ways that

- are built upon purposeful learning objectives,
- enhance students' academic skills, and
- engage learners in relevant processes of self-exploration?

There are a variety of ways teachers can develop instruction and learning so that students are able to trace connections to the hero's journey and make it relevant to their own lives. This, of course, begins with considering texts that are relevant to students and whose heroes are representative of students. Below is an overview of three example classroom approaches to help students make these connections. It is important to acknowledge, of course, there is no one "best" way to do this and that teachers know their students, curriculum, and materials best and are thus best suited to decide which approach lends itself better to their classrooms.

The first strategic approach may rely on Campbell's archetypal hero, the stages of the journey, and characteristics of heroes from different cultures. When outlining and discussing the main stages of the hero's journey—departure, initiation, and return home—teachers need to translate these in terms of relevance to students' lives. Doing so necessitates teachers pose a number of questions to help them get at the "what" and the "why" behind their inclusion of the hero and the concept of the journey in their specific classrooms. Such questions might include:

- What does departure mean?
- When do we cross from one point to another in real life
- What happens during initiation, and is it the point of adolescent struggles and growth?
- What does return home mean and look like?
- And finally, how do people change throughout the journey, and in what ways are those changes contextual, situational, and personal?

These are the types of questions to consider as students are guided through the journey. The major lesson here is that the hero's journey is a journey of self-discovery; it is unique for each individual. Students have to understand that every single person undertakes a distinct path in hopes to find one's purpose, recognize character strengths, and simply understand who this person is or wants to be.

However, unlike the epic journey, individuals' journeys are not final, and after one is over, the next one comes into life because humans constantly face internal or external struggles, make choices, react to situations, and change as a result of decisions and actions. The challenge for teachers, then, is to design instruction that allows students to wrestle with and make sense of these notions.

Another way of teaching the hero's journey and making it relevant to students is by drawing parallels to modern superheroes. Many adolescents read novels and comics and watch films representing such personages. They recognize and connect to these characters, and that recognition can help students analyze and trace the stages of the archetypal hero's journey through engaging, contemporary stories.

Through the study of superheroes, their actions and their journeys, students are also able to recognize and connect to instances of courage, to acts of selflessness, and to a desire to help or save the world and make it a better place. Similarly to epic heroes, modern superheroes often progress through a series of tests, a set of obstacles that make them stronger, preparing them for their final clash with injustice for the greater good of other people.

Two key differences between epic heroes and superheroes, however, are that superheroes, over the years, have become increasingly diverse and that they represent a range of journeys, from large to small, from public to private, creating greater opportunities for student connections. Modern superheroes may also use familiar language and function in a society closely resembling theirs. These traits and the range of heroic characteristics superheroes take up, combined with their popularity, offer powerful and relevant points of entry into students' study of the hero.

This same concept holds true for many motion pictures (often adapted from novels) as well. Students, for example, can also study and connect to heroes found in *Star Wars*, *Harry Potter*, *The Hunger Games*, *The Hobbit*, *The Lord of the Rings*, and so on. One way teachers can layer students' experiences and learning is to connect a variety of these texts (e.g., an epic, a superhero narrative, and a contemporary film) and then task students with drawing similarities and recognizing key differences, which they can then connect back to their own lives.

Regardless of the chosen supplemental text medium—novels, epics, comics, graphic novels, or movies—students should embrace understanding that the hero's quest is life changing, whether for them or for others around them. They should also be provided time and support to make personal connections to these characters and to use their analyses of such heroes and their journeys to reflect on themselves and their personal journeys.

A third possible pedagogical approach is to teach the hero's journey as a journey of self-discovery beginning with contemporary YAL. An example unit following this approach is described in detail in chapter 3. Today's adolescents are more attracted to texts in which they can see themselves and better understand historic, cultural, economic, and developmental values of their own generation. Since students may directly relate to contemporary literary characters' struggles, trials, and challenges, teachers will be able to engage all students, even those who generally express reluctance.

Moreover, this self-exploration will be beneficial to each student's personal growth and help with identity issues along with other teenage challenges associated with anger, bullying, gender, or sexuality. There is a plethora of young adult novels, and each one of them offers insight into a wide range of adolescent experiences. These novels feature diverse characters from different cultural, ethnic, and socioeconomic backgrounds learning about themselves and the world around them.

While the protagonist of the novel described in this, and the subsequent, chapter is a young man, it is also important to highlight stories with girls and young women as leads and to analyze the experiences and contributions of female characters in all texts. To facilitate an exploration of female characters, teachers may consider *Freaky Green Eyes* (Oates, 2003), with a White, seemingly privileged teenager, Franky Pierson who lives in an abusive house ruled by a controlling father and local celebrity, Reid Pierson. Another novel with a strong female heroine is *My Name Is Parvana*, the final book of D. Ellis's *Breadwinner* series, tells a story of a fifteen-year-old girl who lost parents, friends, and a school in a fight for education in post-Taliban Afghanistan.

Among hundreds of other novels with diverse female protagonists, *Sold* (2006) by Patricia McCormick, *Speak* (1999), *Wintergirls* (2009), and *Shout* (2019) by L.H. Anderson, *Hate List* (2009) by J. Brown, *The Hate U Give* by A. Thomas (2017), and *That's Not What Happened* (2018) by K. Keplinger, to name a few, are worth exploring the theme of self-discovery and self-construction.

In the section that follows, we provide one detailed example—Matt de la Peña's *Mexican Whiteboy*—as a way to harness the power of YAL to engage students in personal journeys of self-discovery.

While each of these approaches can be utilized in classrooms separately, they can also be combined to create layered units of instruction. For example, teachers may want to bring in Campbell's archetypal hero as a lens for studying heroes in comics, YAL, and students' contemporary world. For the purposes of this chapter, de la Peña's powerful novel is discussed as a site for students to consider heroic traits and the often complicated nature of adolescent self-discovery. In the subsequent section, de la Peña's novel, *Mexican Whiteboy*, is introduced, connected to the theme of self-journey, and positioned as an anchor text for an instructional unit. Chapter 3, then, offers an example instructional unit for teachers to consider.

NOVEL OVERVIEW: *MEXICAN WHITEBOY* BY MATT DE LA PEÑA

Matt de la Peña's award-winning young adult novel *Mexican Whiteboy* (2008) tells the heartfelt story of Danny Lopez. Angry with his White mother and feeling a need to reunite with his Mexican heritage, sixteen-year-old Danny chooses to spend the summer with his father's relatives in an attempt to get closer to his roots. It doesn't turn out to be easy. As much as he wants to belong, he feels too pale to fit in with his father's family. Furthermore, the young man's identity struggles are complicated by his father's disappearance three years ago, convincing Danny that his "whiteness" is the reason for his father's departure.

Danny doesn't speak much, and, despite his Mexican roots, he doesn't speak Spanish at all, so the only place where the young man feels confident is a baseball field, and it only happens when he is calm and relaxed, which is not very often. His summer starts with a rough scuffle with Uno, a local boy, arrogant and troubled, who cannot let some stranger deliver deadly striking pitches three times in a row. Surprisingly, the boys become friends, and Uno takes Danny under his wing. Together, the two young men try to figure out who they are, what they want, and how to move on with their broken lives.

YAL AND THEMATIC EXPLORATION: *MEXICAN WHITEBOY* AND THE JOURNEY OF SELF-DISCOVERY

Throughout the novel, readers follow Danny Lopez, the protagonist of *Mexican Whiteboy* and his desperate attempt to reconnect with his Mexican roots. At the beginning of the novel, a sixteen-year-old boy is introduced as one who is shy and "aims his eyes at the asphalt" (de la Peña, 2008, p. 2). Right away this description illuminates the inner struggles of the main character. Danny is over six feet tall, and just one year younger than his cousin Sofia, but "he feels like a boy" (p. 2).

Reading this, students may analyze or make connections to Danny by recognizing that something bothers or pains him. They may relate to issues and experiences they have had in their own lives and use those connections to consider both Danny's and their own decisions and actions. The subsequent step in their analysis may be to pose the questions: what makes him feel like this and how does answering that question help them better understand and relate to Danny?

Through reading, students find that Danny Lopez's shyness and lack of confidence stem from his mixed heritage and his internalized views on race. He is "half-Mexican brown." The author presents him as being a shade darker than his peers at Leucadia Prep School in San Diego. He can only see people of the same shade in the lunch line ladies, gardeners, and custodians working on school premises. However, when Danny moves to spend summer with his dad's family in National City, he is very self-conscious of his whiteness because he is a "full shade lighter" than his relatives, "Albino almost" (p. 2). The young man is longing to fit into his father's Mexican family.

Fortunately for Danny, his uncles, aunts, grandparents, and cousins unconditionally accept, love, and support him. They are ready to protect him. However, he finds himself facing another challenge—he does not speak Spanish like everyone else in his father's family. The language barrier becomes even more prominent when the boy meets Liberty, a new girl who came to National City recently. The girl does not speak English at all. It is not easy to have a crush on a girl and be unable to communicate with her. All of these challenges feed Danny's anger at his mom and her way of life.

He blames his mother for his whiteness, for the lack of Mexican culture in the family, and most of all for his father leaving him three years ago as a result. At least, he thinks that the reason his father left him and his younger sister is because he could not continue to surrender to his wife's "White" cultural values. His false assumptions about his father clearly lead to anger with his mother, and it is not until he finally understands his family, including his father, that he better understands his mother and ultimately better understands himself.

Yet another important character in Danny's life journey is Uno. Danny and Uno bond over baseball and various other teenage interests, but perhaps most of all, they bond over internal struggles with who they are. They both seem to feel their lives would be better if they were more like the other. Because of this, they balance each other out, recognize they have quite a bit in common, and ultimately help the other to accept who they are. That is, they help one another through the rocky journey of self-discovery.

Without that support, they may have each remained stagnant in and frustrated with their lives. Danny and Uno's relationship opens up the opportunity for students to critique the often taught hero narrative by questioning whether or not the hero's journey is or must be taken alone (like Beowulf and Odysseus, for instance). In many cases, friends, family, and other support groups play vital roles in these journeys and in the heroic acts often perceived to be undertaken by individuals.

Danny's identity struggles are complicated by societal definitions and labels that impact the world in which he lives. In his world, labels, such as "White," "Brown," "Mexican," and "biracial" dictate a person's place in society, and in Danny's case, he sees this as impacting how he is viewed within his family, at school, on the baseball diamond, etc.

Mexican Whiteboy illustrates how two major characters, like so many other young adults, find their identity to be messy, often confusing, and yet evolving. For example, while Danny is trying to come to terms with his racial/ethnic identity, the book also deals with much more—a journey that includes dealing with anger, violence, and self-harm. The novel and characters reaffirm to young people that identity is not a fixed label. Teens are able to change and grow as their knowledge and understanding of themselves, and the world around them, helps them in developing strong values and beliefs.

Teachers may see many young readers connecting to Danny and this novel in a myriad of ways because it offers hope to those readers who may feel they live in seemingly hopeless situations. A skillful writer, de la Peña offers a glimpse of the future through his characters; both Danny and Uno have the courage to move beyond the situations that have previously defined them. They are willing to take risks, and they constantly question their own situations.

One way students may examine Danny and Uno's development in the novel and the ways they can connect to the characters is to consider how individuals position themselves separately and in relation to others around them (e.g., their family, friends, and the community). In other words, one goal of teaching de la Peña's novel might be to help students begin to think about what it is that makes them unique individuals and what it is that connects them to others in their lives.

Finally, the novel study may help teachers to begin frank conversations about racial struggles in this country and the world and how to promote anti-racism. This might be the right point to consider and advance students' knowledge about abolitionist movements, human rights, racial discrimination, and privilege and to develop further understanding of the concepts of equality and equity.

KEY IDEAS

This chapter introduces the first universal theme—the journey of self-discovery, often taught as the hero's journey—and discusses ways it has often been taught in the past, including the ways students are tasked with studying and making sense of the theme. Additionally, it shares a variety of ways these traditional approaches fall short of connecting to the diverse students populating contemporary classrooms.

Next, the chapter offers a glimpse into how the hero's journey can be reconceptualized as plural and individualized journeys of self-discovery. It suggests possible ways that invite students to make meaningful connections with characters and experiences and use these connections to better understand who they are as individuals while carefully guiding them along their own paths of self-discovery.

Lastly, it discusses one YAL text, Matt de la Peña's *Mexican Whiteboy*, as a method for engaging students in the study of the journey of self-discovery. To frame this, a summary of the novel is provided. As an example for teachers, the chapter presents the ways *Mexican Whiteboy* connects to the theme and proposes a useful starting point for students' explorations.

The following chapter presents readers with an outline of an instructional unit using de la Peña's novel to foster literary study around the journey of self-discovery and, by connection, an exploration into their own self-identities.

Chapter 3

Conceptual Teaching Unit

Identity Exploration on the Way to Self-Discovery

This conceptual teaching unit is developed for a ninth grade English language arts class. Since this is an example of a teaching unit, it is created keeping in mind a certain grade-level, that of a high school English I class in this case. However, teachers may take this unit as a foundation for constructing units at the middle-school level. Students in grades six through eight will benefit from self-explorations as it may ease their way to high school and help with understanding the ways they are in control of their own self-development and the voices they have in choosing who they want to be.

While the student population of any classroom is diverse in a variety of ways, many teens at this age experience similar challenges and issues as part of their identity development. At fourteen or fifteen years of age, students find themselves at an intersection—simultaneously occupying spaces of adolescence and adulthood with all the stresses that accompany each individually and that go along with such growth. Adolescents are constantly bombarded with pressures from outside influences, such as their parents, the media, their peers, society, their community, and even their teachers.

Sadly, along with age-related adolescent issues, educators have also to take into consideration individual lives and struggles of their students. There might be teenagers in their classrooms who have been denied a childhood and adolescence altogether through poverty, homelessness, loss of parents, bullying, and physical, emotional, or sexual abuse. Some may even live independently, making it more difficult to provide for themselves and attain the daily necessities many consider simple and take for granted.

A teacher's job is not only to teach literature but also to help students use literature as a way to navigate their own lives and to negotiate the pressures surrounding them daily. A unit focused around the theme of self-discovery, or identity search, can assist them in this endeavor. The five-week unit described below is designed to help students connect with literary characters and use those connections to better understand who they are as humans and as teens, and their places within the world, within their families, and within their schools and communities.

Another great lesson for students is to come to a realization that they are also and always in the process of self-construction. Their development is constant, and they hold considerable control over who they want to become. One of the larger ideas is to understand how external influences also shape individuality and how individuals and their actions affect people around them.

Because teachers know their students, schools, and curricula best, they are best suited to place an instructional unit devoted to exploring the theme of self-discovery wherever they see fit. In this chapter, however, the unit is described as the second of an academic year. Such placement is for three main reasons. First, it allows for space at the beginning of the year for English teachers to learn more about their students, including their interests, home lives, school experiences, and academic progress, thus helping them plan a more efficient and relevant unit on self-discovery.

Second, teachers may want to use an opening unit to build and activate background knowledge through students' experiences in middle school, around heroes and journeys, and using short stories to build their capacity to analyze longer literary texts. Moreover, teachers can use this background knowledge building to scaffold students as they approach critical thinking and writing about personal development.

Third, positioning this as the second unit is intended to aid students in developing their own identities early in the year, which they will then apply as lenses to all subsequent units and thematic study. It is also anticipated that a lot of independent reading of self-selected texts is going on, beyond the material that has been or will be taught in class. Students are consistently encouraged to reflect on the books they are currently reading for pleasure and/or their favorite books in their past.

The unit described in this chapter builds on the discussion of relevancy via YAL in chapter 2. The texts chosen for this unit are carefully selected to offer students a wide range of viewpoints and perspectives of adolescents and young adults from a variety of walks of life. The anchor text of this unit is *Mexican Whiteboy* (2008) by Matt de la Peña. This young adult novel tells a story of sixteen-year-old Danny Lopez, who is trying to figure out who he is and how his biracial background affects his life and his view of himself. Students will also be reading, discussing, and analyzing a variety of short stories, poems, song lyrics, articles, and video clips that provide some aspect of adolescent struggles with identity development and other issues connected to growth, development, and maturation.

Adolescent readers view characters in YA novels as living and wrestling with real problems close to their own life experiences as teens (Bean & Rigoni, 2001). In other words, they are better able to see themselves in these characters. At the center of most YA novels are questions of personal development, or self-construction, including value systems and how teens position themselves within communities. When students begin to understand that their seemingly unique, teenage experiences are actually quite common, they realize there is a place for them in the world.

A variety of activities for this unit are tailored to allow students to become confident with reading, thinking critically, and with forming their own conclusions about a text and themselves through oral and written tasks. To help cultivate this growth in their skills, students will be reading, participating in daily journaling to trace thoughts about their personal journeys of self-discovery, completing small-group and individual projects, and sharing their views during class discussions.

The major assessments for the unit include pre- and post-assessments to let teachers evaluate what students know about identity and how it affects their lives before engaging in unit readings and activities. The culminating assessment for the unit is a personal narrative (described below) in which students will demonstrate their progress toward understanding the concepts of identity, self-discovery, and self-acceptance. While completing this task, students will undergo all steps of the writing process, including prewriting, drafting, revision and editing, publication and presentation along with percolating (Romano, 2004) throughout the process.

OVERARCHING CONCEPTS, ESSENTIAL QUESTIONS, AND UNIT OBJECTIVES

Two major overarching concepts for this teaching unit are identity and identity development. Throughout the unit, together with a teacher and following literary characters from the novel, using poetry, nonfiction excerpts, and video selections, students will embark on a journey toward self-discovery. They will listen, read, think, and write about the adolescent characters and about themselves.

This unit builds on student knowledge of the quest, as discussed in chapter 2. By this time, students are most likely familiar with some epic literature and archetypal heroes. Applying their previous knowledge, with teachers' guidance, students will be able to draw connections from the hero's journey to a journey of self-discovery. Reading and analyzing a contemporary young adult text, they will understand how literature reflects life and how they may see themselves within and through literature. They will recognize that, regardless of whether their journey is physical or metaphysical, they need patience, perseverance, insight, and support to gain wisdom and experience along the way. Students will explore how people often assign value to their lives through achievements and failures and the costs of giving in to impulse, temptation, and anger.

More importantly, students can begin to understand that their identities are not fixed; they are constantly evolving and changing based on their actions and experiences. Moreover, they learn that this evolution is normal and healthy and that it is a vital component to their becoming. They learn from their experiences, take risks, and influence people (and are influenced by people) around them. Their quest will be guided by the following questions:

- Who am I? Who gets to decide?
- What is my place at home, school, or in society?
- In what ways is my identity fluid? What factors influence this?
- How do my actions affect other people, and how do others affect me?
- Do I dare to disturb a universe?
- How does understanding more about myself help me grow, develop, and understand the world around me?

Along with critical thinking about the overarching concepts and essential questions, students will be able to enhance their academic analytical and writing skills. These skills may be drawn from the academic standards used in each state. By the end of the unit, students should be able to:

- Read and understand complex texts
- Cite relevant textual evidence that supports analysis
- Identify one or more themes in literary works
- Analyze theme development through point of view, settings, and plot
- Analyze how complex characters develop over the course of a text
- Recognize irony and its effect on story and character development
- Compose well-developed and constructed responses to texts
- Develop a personal narrative using narrative techniques and sensory details
- Demonstrate use of the writing process to strengthen writing
- Write for different lengths of time for a range of tasks
- Participate in a variety of whole-class and small-group discussions about the text
- Understand academic vocabulary
- Demonstrate command of the conventions of Standard English when writing
- Demonstrate ability to use a variety of sentence structures

The next section presents a calendar plan for the entire unit that helps teachers map out the major instructional strategies, activities, and assessments in a logical progression.

CALENDAR PLAN FOR A CONCEPTUAL TEACHING UNIT

Before planning any teaching unit for a secondary ELA classroom in detail in the form of daily lesson plans, it is essential to create a calendar plan (unit) at a glance, showing possible activities, projects, or teaching strategies for the day and due dates for unit assignments and homework. It also demonstrates that teachers incorporate a range of different instructional strategies which are sequenced in order to achieve understanding of the unit's overarching concepts and essential questions and to reach the set objectives.

This calendar plan presents a mapped out unit considering students' prior knowledge and understandings about the theme. It begins with a pre-assessment and initial exploration of the theme through reflective journaling, class discussion, and response to poetry. Gradually students build on previous learning experiences, embarking on their journeys to learn about the author, engage in reading, discussion, and writing about the novel, and think about personal development.

Throughout the unit, close reading of the anchor text is supplemented with poems, short stories, nonfiction pieces, and short video clips. Students complete small-group and individual projects leading them to advanced thematic analysis. They also work on strengthening academic skills, such as citing textual evidence, making inferences, taking notes and annotating, identifying theme(s) and tracing their development, improving narrative techniques in writing, etc. By the end of the unit, students will write the final reflective journal and create a personal narrative to demonstrate their development across the unit and their understanding of unit objectives.

Tables 3.1–3.5 present an example calendar plan for a five-week unit exploring the theme of self-discovery. Each week briefly outlines daily class activities and assignments to create a sequenced progression toward completing the unit objectives and culminating assessments. This calendar plan is flexible; that is, teachers may adopt it partially or adjust it to their students' needs. They may also use pacing that best suits students in the classroom. For example, eighth graders may take up to three weeks for reading the novel, and some projects may take two days instead of one.

Week 1 introduces students to the unit theme, major assignments, and projects. Since the unit is centered on the theme of self-discovery and helps students embark on their personal identity search journeys, they begin with

Table 3.1 Week 1 of the Teaching Unit

Day	Activities
Monday	Reflective Journal 1: Who are you? How would you introduce yourself to a new friend? Pre-Assessment: Anticipatory set with essential questions for the unit. What is Identity? Initial class discussion *Endless Search,* a poem by Alonzo Lopez—reading and response reflection Introduction to the Unit
Tuesday	Reflective Journal 2: Who are your friends? What kind of people are they? Building background knowledge: Matt de la Peña and his novels. Introducing a novel, *Mexican Whiteboy*—book trailer Making inferences about the novel development Homework: read pp. 1–28 of the novel
Wednesday	Reflective Journal 3: What makes you unique (from family, friends, community members, etc.)? Reading and discussion of *Mexican Whiteboy:* setting and its function *Say Something* strategy introduction and modeling Danny's portrait at a glance—a short, constructed response Homework: read pp. 29–57
Thursday	Reflective Journal 4: Who are your heroes (from real life, movies, or literature)? What characteristics do they have that you find heroic? Reading and discussion of *Mexican Whiteboy:* characters Close reading with follow-up discussion strategy Introducing Cornell Notes "Sorry for not being a stereotype" by Rita Pyrillis Homework: read pp. 58–82
Friday	Reflective Journal 5: What have you learned about yourself throughout this week, considering our readings, your reflective journals, and class discussions? Reading and discussion of *Mexican Whiteboy:* character analysis Citing relevant textual evidence Homework: read pp. 83–136 (since this is for the weekend, they may read more)

reflective journal writing and continue it throughout the unit as a tool for learning with literary characters about themselves. During the first day of the unit, students complete an anticipatory set serving as a pre-assessment of students' understanding of the overarching unit concepts and essential questions.

Further, the first week presents a writer, Matt de la Peña and his novel *Mexican Whiteboy*. As students read the novel, they begin discussions to analyze setting and characters, and conduct close reading of selected passages to assist with locating textual evidence and character analysis. Two helpful literacy strategies—*Say Something* and Cornell Notes—are also presented during the first week.

Table 3.2 Week 2 of the Teaching Unit

Monday	Reflective Journal 6: Which character from *Mexican Whiteboy* do you most relate to? How are you relating to them? In what ways are you similar? Reading and discussing *Mexican Whiteboy:* narration and point of view Small-group *Analyzing Song Lyrics Activity* Homework: read pp.137–163
Tuesday	Reflective Journal 7: How might your own image of yourself be different from what others see in you? Reading and discussion of *Mexican Whiteboy:* identifying themes Cornell Notes Homework: read pp. 164–189
Wednesday	Reflective Journal 8: How does your name represent who you are? In other words, what does or doesn't it say about you? Reading and discussion of *Mexican Whiteboy:* analysis of theme development Cornell Notes Homework: read pp. 190–213
Thursday	Reflective Journal 9: How do you use your voice to express yourself? And how does your voice represent who you are? Reading and discussion of *Mexican Whiteboy:* author's choices concerning how to structure a text and order events Homework: read pp. 214–225
Friday	Reflective Journal 10: What have you learned about yourself throughout this week, considering our readings, your reflective journals, and class discussions? How has your learning about yourself changed from the previous week? Reading and Discussing *Mexican Whiteboy:* pivotal moments in Danny's journey *Character Identity Web,* a small-group work Homework: read pp. 226–247 (complete the novel)

The major focus of Week 2 is reading and further discussion of the novel. Along with that, students continue writing reflectively in response to daily prompts. They also progress with Cornell Notes. At the end of the week, students work on a small-group project creating a Character Identity Web. They are to finish reading the novel during the weekend as homework. All of these activities aim to advance students' understanding of the overarching unit concepts and are geared toward the unit's final project—narrative writing.

The third week of the unit begins, similarly to weeks one and two, with reflective writing and a culminating theme discussion. The week is filled with enrichment activities. Students present their Character Identity Web and work on a community identity project and a letter to Danny's father. They will enhance their understanding of irony by reading a short story by Chopin and compose a literary analysis essay based on the discussions and small projects completed in class.

Table 3.3 Week 3 of the Teaching Unit

Monday	Reflective Journal 11: How do your childhood memories help shape your identity? How have you grown from your previous experiences? *Poem Full of Worry Ending with My Birth* by Tarfia Faizullah Discussing *Mexican Whiteboy:* culminating discussion of themes and *Character Identity Web* group-work presentations *Community Identity Project* introduction Socratic Seminar introduction
Tuesday	Reflective Journal 12: If you are starring in a movie, what kind of a character would you be? And how would that character represent who you are? In-class character analysis essay based on *Character Identity Web Community Identity Project*
Wednesday	Reflective Journal 13: How do physical appearance and personality impact identity? *Desiree's Baby* by Kate Chopin, an irony mini-lesson Complete character analysis essay
Thursday	Reflective Journal 14: What are your interests, hobbies, and passions? What do they tell about who you are? Questioning the author: students questions to Matt de la Peña Creative mini-project: a letter to Danny's father
Friday	Reflective Journal 15: What have you learned about yourself throughout this week, considering our readings, your reflective journals, and class discussions? How has your learning about yourself changed from previous weeks? *Community Identity Project* presentations

Continuing self-discovery explorations, Week 4 offers a range of after-reading activities. The week begins with introduction of a culminating, personal narrative assignment, on which students work for the duration of the remaining two weeks. Students review and refresh their knowledge of the writing process and 6+1 traits of writing, completing several prewriting gateway activities. Along with the writing, they will read a short story and an excerpt from nonfiction literary text and listen to a TED Talk to further examine issues centered around personal identity development.

Finally, Week 5 is primarily devoted to writing. The teacher facilitates each day's writing session by assisting students with their needs during drafting, revision, and editing steps. Students briefly overview common usage errors, continue to learn how to provide effective and constructive feedback to peers, and how to address peer's comments and suggestions. The unit concludes with a post-assessment evaluating their understanding of the overarching unit concepts and essential questions. A final reflective journal and a personal narrative demonstrate students' progress in the journey of self-discovery.

Identity Exploration on the Way to Self-Discovery 37

Table 3.4 Week 4 of the Teaching Unit

Monday	Reflective Journal 16: What mood(s) are you in today? What roles does mood play in our identity (how we see ourselves and how others see us)? How does our mood influence our choices and decisions? Introducing personal narrative *Birthday Box*, a short story by Jane Yolen
Tuesday	Reflective Journal 17: Yesterday you wrote about mood. For today, how do your emotions dictate your behavior and who you are? *The Danger of a Single Story* by Adichie, C. N. (2009). TED Talk
Wednesday	Reflective Journal 18: Do you affect people around you? Do they affect you? In what ways? For example, how does conflict help us on our journeys of self-discovery? Drawing connections—"Understanding Strangers" (pp. 10–14) from *Stories of Identity* Sensory details lesson: analyze de la Peña's narrative techniques through select passages Prewriting 1: A Senses Poem
Thursday	Reflective Journal 19: How do you handle stress? What helps you relax and/or calm down anxiety? Sharing autobiographical life maps in small groups Prewriting 2: Treasure Activity
Friday	Reflective Journal 20: What have you learned about yourself throughout this week, considering our readings, your reflective journals, and class discussions? How has your learning about yourself changed from previous weeks? 6+1 Traits of writing Attention to an intended audience Initial drafting of personal narrative

Table 3.5 Week 5 of the Teaching Unit

Monday	Attention to language: review common usage errors Drafting 2—continue drafting the personal narrative Homework: Complete the first draft. Prepare it for a peer review session

Tuesday	Providing constructive feedback
	Peer Review Session:
	    Round 1: reading for content
	    Round 2: evaluating organization and structure
	    Round 3: emphasis on coherence, flow, diction, and sentence structure
	    Round 4: attention to grammar, usage, and mechanics

Wednesday	Revisions and Editing Homework: Complete suggested revisions and edits, prepare the narrative for the final submission
Thursday	Post-Assessment: extended response to essential questions of the pre-assessment Small-group discussion: Think-Pair-Share student responses to essential questions
Friday	Final Reflective Journal 21: Who am I? What is my place at home, among peers, and in society? Respond to this question considering what we read, discussed, and what you understand about yourself as of today Final drafts submissions, presentation, and reflections on writing

FOSTERING THEMATIC ANALYSIS OF SELF-DISCOVERY: SAMPLE ACTIVITIES FOR ELA CLASSROOMS

Below are examples of instructional activities teachers can use throughout this unit on the journey of self-discovery. This section is organized in two ways. First, activities are categorized as introductory or taking place before reading begins, useful during reading, and designed for post reading. Second, for each activity, there is (1) an overview of the activity and (2) a discussion of how and why it connects to the novel, *Mexican Whiteboy*, and/or the larger unit goals.

Teachers are, of course, best suited to make instructional decisions for their own students, and there are undoubtedly many other valuable learning experiences and activities that can be used in this unit. Teachers may use, modify or create similar, more effective activities considering their students, classrooms, and instructional goals. The activities suggested here are intended to serve as examples and help teachers think about how to organize and develop their own thematic studies.

Introductory Activities

It is helpful to begin any exploration of the journey of self-discovery with activities to build background knowledge. Teachers may consider various ways of introducing a new unit. Since students will be tackling issues of self-discovery and struggles associated with this journey, an anticipatory set with essential questions for the unit may assess what they know and how they feel about the overarching concept of identity and self-development. Teachers may adopt and use the questions suggested in the Overarching Concepts, Essential Questions, and Unit Objectives section or develop their own questions based on the specific groups of students they teach.

This initial activity does not just assess the prior knowledge, but responding to the questions also prepares students for thoughtful reading and discussion of *Mexican Whiteboy*, as well as draws critical connections to personal experiences. From the first lesson of the unit, they will think, form understanding, and write about their personal journey.

A follow-up discussion of these questions will ultimately lead explicitly to the concept of "identity." It may start with a direct question "What is identity?" and continue with questions, such as:

- In what ways is identity unique to individuals? What about groups?
- How do we know who we are? And what factors contribute to answering that question?

- When and how do we first know (or hear) who we are (i.e., how does what others tell us impact how we see ourselves)?
- In what ways can an identity be imposed on us by others?
- Can people have multiple identities?

The goal with these is to provide students space to wrestle with these questions and with their own understanding of identity. Students may initially struggle to think and write deeply around these concepts and may, as a result, provide surface-level or stock responses, especially at the beginning of the unit. Used formatively, these responses can inform teachers on the levels of scaffolding and support necessary as students move into and through the thematic unit. Similarly, initial answers to these questions can serve as self-assessment for students, both in the moment and across the unit. Students, for example, can consider what they currently know and understand about identity. Additionally, they may revisit their responses later to assess their learning and growth.

As another step of the introductory lesson, teachers may present a five-line poem by Alonzo Lopez titled *Endless Search*. The speaker of this poem complains to be "forever searching" and being unable to complete this quest despite the constant effort. This poem exemplifies the speaker's struggles to identify and understand oneself and appeals to adolescents prompting their search for themselves. It also serves as a proper segue to introduce a unit on a journey of self-discovery and Matt de la Peña's novel *Mexican Whiteboy* (2008). From this point and throughout the unit, students, with the teacher's guidance, will initiate their expedition into a world of self-discovery.

Reading and Discussing the Novel

Reflective Journal

Throughout the entire unit, students will keep a reflective journal. They will write in it every day, except for the last week of the unit, when they work on their personal narrative assignment. Daily prompts, posted on the board by the teacher, will ask students to respond to questions or situations that help them understand themselves by clarifying their positions, values, and beliefs. These one-page journal entries at the beginning of each lesson will also ask students to reflect on and connect with the novel characters. Sample journal prompts include:

- Who are you? How would you introduce yourself to a new friend?
- Who are your friends? What kind of people are they?
- Which character from *Mexican Whiteboy* do you most relate to? How are you relating to them? In what ways are you similar?
- How do you handle stress? What helps you relax and/or calm down anxiety?

Some of the questions suggested for reflective journaling might be sensitive, and even painful, to students. It is important to remember that students may come from violent or dysfunctional homes or foster care. There may be students who are bullied or those who have experienced shunning, displacement, or other harmful actions from those around them, all impacting how and if they make friends. These serve as examples of why teachers should use knowledge of their students to modify and adjust questions.

It is helpful also to explain that students have to write their entries as a self-exploration tool, but they are not required to share openly in class and have the right to keep their journals private. After completing each journal, teachers invite students to discuss the daily prompt and connect it to the novel or any other supplemental reading for the day.

These thoughtful daily reflections become a springboard for continuing discussion and thematic analysis, allow students to explore themselves along with analysis and interpretation of the novel characters, and, at the same time, prepare students for their culminating assignment—the personal narrative. Moreover, completing routine, short writing on a daily basis assists in planning and developing longer projects as well as strengthening writing skills.

Say Something Strategy

Say Something is a helpful strategy that keeps students' focus on reading and encourages them to respond to the text. It is especially effective when students work in small groups of three or four. For example, the teacher assigns a page or two of the text to read and discuss in class. This may be a passage from a novel, any supplemental short story, or a piece of nonfiction. Students read the text out loud in groups taking turns. They stop occasionally to comment on what they have read—to "say something." The other group members comment on the first person's comment, thus there is a discussion within a group, which can be followed by a whole-class discussion of the text. It becomes less intimidating to talk in class after a small-group discussion practice.

Some readers struggle to say something even in small-group settings, so teachers may help by providing sentence starters to comment, predict, question, or make connections. There are a few examples of sentence starters in table 3.6 to assist students in response to the text.

Teachers may revise or completely change sentence starters depending on the goals for a specific text discussion. They may use time or place modifiers, chronological, problem-solution, or cause and effect sentence structures to emphasize the focus of the text, discussion, and lesson objectives. The main goal of the strategy is to get students talking and sharing their insights and positions, which they will ultimately apply to their analyses of the novel.

Table 3.6 Sentence Starters for *Say Something Strategy*

Make a Comment:	Make a Prediction:
This is interesting because. . .	I think that. . .
It seems to me that. . .	My prediction is that. . .
My favorite part is. . .	Since ___ happened, I think ___ will happen
I don't quite understand how. . .	What if. . .
Ask a question:	**Make a Connection:**
What does this part about. . . mean?	The differences between the characters are like. . .
How would ___ act if ___ happens?	
Do you think that. . .?	The main character behaves like. . .
Why did ___ act like this?	I used to think this way. . .
Why did the author. . .?	This episode reminds me of. . .

Character Identity Web—Small-Group Work

By the end of the second week of the unit, when reading of the novel is almost complete, students are prepared to work on the *Character Identity Web*. This is a small-group project with three or four students in each group. It is possible to complete within thirty minutes of one class period and present it during the next class. Each group is assigned or may choose a character from *Mexican Whiteboy*—Danny, Uno, Uncle Ray, Sofia, Liberty, or Wendy—and create a web trying to represent that character's identity as thoroughly as possible based on the information from the novel.

Developing this identity web, students have to illustrate various characteristics of the chosen personage which include but are not limited to

- appearance,
- ethnicity and/or culture,
- family and friends,
- habits and practices,
- hobbies and interests,
- objects and possessions, and
- beliefs, values, and choices.

These are characteristics that help determine people's identity and understanding of their behavior and life choices. Completing this task, students will also, even if subconsciously, think about their own identity constructs. They will have to think about family, friends, school and home community, and how these affect their beliefs, values, and choices. Thus, following the novel characters in their journeys of discovery, students will engage in their own self-exploration.

Students will also notice how one characteristic intersects with and influences the others. For example, Danny Lopez's appearance hints on his interests and is directly connected to his ethnic background and family. The author narrates him as being "a shade over six foot," long and thin "with skinny arms hanging down skinny thighs" (de la Peña, 2008, p. 2). This is the reason Danny is able to throw impressive fastballs.

Further, readers find the description of the boy's skin color, which leads us to his biracial family and ethnic background. He is a "shade darker than all the white kids" at his prep school and a "full shade lighter" than the Mexican side of his family. Figure 3.1 provides an example of a complete Character Identity Map of Danny Lopez.

Together, appearance, family, friends, and interests affect Danny's behavior, his values, beliefs, and choices. He is very shy, almost to the point of not speaking at all when he is around other peers or adults. The young man is convinced that his father's side of the family is better for him, so he decides to spend summer with them instead of with his mother, sister, and a potential step-father. He desires to reconnect with dad and develops a plan to earn money and go to Mexico. Students may find other important connections by analyzing Danny's relationships with friends.

Based on the *Character Identity Web*, students may participate in classroom discussions, compose a character analysis essay, and prepare for a final writing project—a personal narrative of self-discovery. Most importantly, they will keep thinking about their personal development and struggles associated with it.

Community Identity Project

To help facilitate their journeys of self-discovery, students can conduct a community identity project. The goal here is to better understand those around them, the areas in which they live and interact, and how those communities play roles in shaping who they are as individuals. As part of the process, students will engage in critical thinking about their communities and the issues impacting them.

This will help students to better know those in their community circle and to better understand the culture, history, and identities influencing their lives. Moreover, they will inquire and answer questions about what it means to be part of a community—a sense of belonging is part of developing one's own identity.

Through interactions and interviews, students ask community members what their journeys to self-discovery looked like and included. Sample interview questions might include: What role(s) has the community played in becoming who you are? Which community members (e.g., family, friends, neighbors, teachers, etc.), specifically, have contributed to your growth and development? In what ways do you believe you've impacted your community? Working with students to compose a list of possible questions can help provide focus and clarity before sending them out on their own.

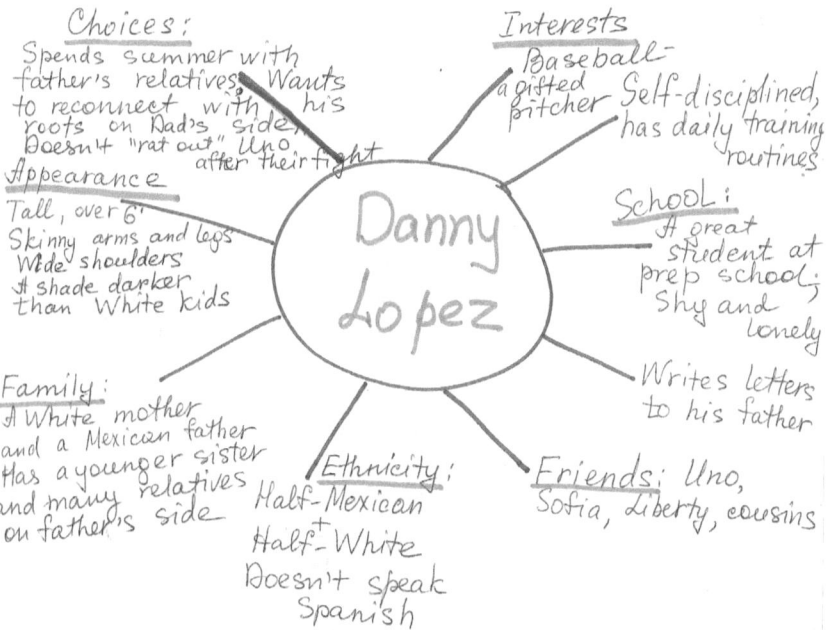

Figure 3.1 Danny's Identity Map. *Source*: Authors.

As part of the process, students can document the interviews by taking notes and photographs, by recording the conversations, through reflections immediately after, and so forth. The goal here is to provide students with tools to collect information that they can then return to as they reflect, write, and learn from the experiences.

Compiling a database of family, friends, neighbors, and so forth, and then conducting interviews with them can provide a nuanced and layered lens for viewing themselves and as points of contact for their journeys. To help students make connections to the novel, they can also use the interview experiences they have to more fully consider Danny's identity development and the role(s) community plays influencing it as they work toward their own narratives of self-discovery.

While students can certainly choose to observe and interview a variety of people and spaces, it may serve them well to focus on a smaller number of those they believe have influenced their lives and development. Teachers can work with students to brainstorm lists of community members, interview questions, observation protocols, and so on.

Teachers are, of course, best suited to make these decisions for their own classrooms, but requiring some version of a final product (e.g., essay, mini-portfolio, or community profile, followed by a presentation) can be useful in ensuring students synthesize and make meaning from the process. For the unit described in this chapter, students will present their findings to the class.

Enrichment Activities

Analyzing Narrative Techniques

To prepare students for writing a narrative, teachers need to organize some groundwork toward strengthening the use of narrative techniques. One effective approach is to improve writing by examining skillfully written narratives. Thus, analyzing de la Peña's narrative techniques and then practicing them independently can be helpful. To conduct such a lesson, teachers have to choose three to five passages from *Mexican Whiteboy* that demonstrate the writer's skills to use language to tell a story and convey ideas.

Table 3.7 provides examples of passages that teachers may suggest for analysis of narrative techniques. Teachers may model the first passage analysis, explaining that students have to pay attention to de la Peña's use of words and phrases, sentence structures, sensory details, or imagery, creating rich descriptions of reflective nature based on characters' experiences and observations. After that, students may work in small groups to analyze two or three passages, and finally, each student may respond to one passage in writing individually. For example, a teacher may offer the following passage:

> Back in Leucadia, [Danny] made a pact with himself. No more words. Or as few as he could possibly get away with. When his dad spoke at all, he mostly spoke Spanish, but Danny never learned. All he had was his mom's English. And he didn't want that anymore. Up in Leucadia it was easy. Nobody paid him any attention anyway because he was Mexican. He roamed the school halls with his head down like a ghost. Drifted in and out of classrooms without a peep. Nobody even saw him as a real person. But down here, where everybody's skin is dark, everybody seems to be coming at him. (pp. 16–17)

In this passage, the narrator is revealing Danny's thoughts about himself and even more so the thoughts of others about him, and how their views make him feel. It seems to him that no one pays attention to him when he is at his prep school, but somehow attention shifts when he finds himself among the Mexicans. His liminal position in both spaces urges him to develop a defensive mechanism. He decides not to talk much, to the point that some people think he is mute. De la Peña skillfully employs this into his narrative.

To analyze further, readers witness short, almost choppy sentences and sentence fragments, some of them beginning with conjunctions or prepositions not quite "suited" to begin a sentence, for example: "And he didn't want it anymore," or "Drifted in and out of classrooms without a peep."

Table 3.7 Suggested Passages from *Mexican Whiteboy* to Analyze de la Peña's Narrative Techniques

Passage	Narrative Techniques
Angela and Bee comb Danny over with their almond-shaped eyes, devour his out-of-place surfer style like a pack of rabid dogs. Danny cringes at how different he must seem to his cousin friends. They're all dark chocolate colored, hair sprayed up, dressed in pro jerseys and Dickies, Timberlands. Gold and silver chains. Calligraphy-style tats. Danny's skin is too clean, too light, his clothes too soft. (p. 3)	Use of active verbs: comb, devour, and cringe Sensory language: almond-shaped, chocolate-covered Parallel structures: too clean, too light, and too soft
Uno glances up at the tracks, shakes his arm out and stretches his neck. "Trains got crazy power," he says. "Sometimes I think about that. . . when someone steps to me in a fight. I think how I stood under this bridge and held on to this pole and took all that train power into my body. It's the power then it ain't really me that's fighting no more. It's the power of the train coming outta my body. And ain't nobody gonna mess with that kind of power, right?" (p. 147)	Reflection Use of vernacular
Then it all poured out of his mouth. "I'm so happy right now. Being here with you. In National City. I came here because sometimes I feel like a fake Mexican. And I don't want to be a fake. I wanna be real. I love my dad's family. And I love the culture and the language and everything gramma cooks and the way they live. I've always wished I was more like them. But it's twice as bad since my dad left. . . . I wish I could tell you how pretty I think you are in Spanish. But I can't. Because I never learned." (p. 188)	Effective use of short, abrupt sentences, creating a sense of urgency
"It was like she was saying it to more than just her parents, though. She was saying it to everybody around her that day. To the whole world, even. 'Here I come.' And I kept thinking, Man, I bet I was like that when I was little, too. What's happened to me since then? We all start out believing we can do anything. Even Mexican kids that grow up here. But at some point we lose it. It totally disappears. Like me, for example. Why is that?" (p. 212)	Reflection and questioning

This passage helps readers understand Danny's struggles with his ethnic background, or "lack of being Mexican" enough. He feels that he is lost and doesn't belong to his surroundings. It also explains his shyness and desire to be unnoticed whether he is in his school or among the cousins and their friends in National City.

The narrative analysis of the passage may be followed by a writing practice, in which students attempt to imitate the passage they analyzed and write about one of their own memories. For example, their imitation efforts may result in a passage similar to this:

Mom's house was relaxed. Hardly any rules to follow. I could do whatever I wanted. Dad's house was strict. The rules were hard to follow. And it didn't matter what I wanted. But they both said they were trying their best. Right! I was too young to understand the why and the how. My brother and I were just confused. At least we had each other. Moving each week. Back and forth. Rules, no rules. We were guests in someone else's house. But we were together.

While not an exact imitation, this passage effectively employs short, abrupt sentences and fragments that help readers understand the narrator's inner turmoil of being split between two parents and trying to adjust to each place with established routines and expectations for behavior. What makes this example interesting is that it does not have any obvious imagery, only hinting at the situation and surroundings, but nonetheless creates a vivid description.

Sensory Details Activity

As one of the prewriting activities toward a personal narrative project, teachers may engage students in a six-minute sensory details exercise writing a *Senses Poem* (Bolton, 2014). In this poem, students have to write a line for each of the senses: sight, smell, sound, taste, touch, and feeling. They may choose one object or person to describe, or use different objects, people, or a combination of both. If students are able to come up with their own line progression, they may work independently. Students who need scaffolding might be provided with a template similar to this one:

Yesterday I saw . . . (add an object or person and at least two descriptive modifiers)
It (she, he) smelled like . . . (describe a smell)
I heard . . . (describe a sound)
I imagined it tasted like . . . (describe a taste)
It was . . . to a touch (describe a touch)
I felt . . . (describe a feeling)

This exercise targets the use of imagery and pushes students to use precise words and phrases that describe objects or people and their attributes, and ultimately a feeling that these objects or people evoke. They may modify the template as long as they attempt to describe all six senses. The result may read similar to this:

Yesterday I saw a rose, first, bright-yellow,
It smelled like mom's favorite perfume, gentle and pleasant.
I heard a wind, briskly and wild,
I imagined it tasted like salt, sharp and edgy.
The wind touched the rose, biting its petals,
I felt pain, acute and agonizing.

Prewriting exercises improve writing skills, and this one addresses word choices. Often students struggle to describe their feelings or thoughts. To assist, teachers may suggest students use online dictionaries to look for words describing a certain sense. Many of the feelings students describe and write about can connect to their own personal stories; as such, they can pull from small writing activities, such as the sensory detail activity, to strengthen their personal narrative projects.

A Personal Narrative Writing Project

As one of the culminating activities for this unit, students will be asked to use their experiences across the unit to compose their own narrative of self-discovery. Throughout their thematic study, students will use *Mexican Whiteboy* to relate to others, to develop empathy, and to better understand themselves as individuals. Ultimately, their ongoing analysis of Danny's (and other characters') experiences will serve as a sort of mentor text that will help them to write their own narratives. Additionally, the reflective journaling students complete can also become fuel for their self-discovery narratives. In these entries, students draw on their own developing analyses of the text, the questions they posed and the predictions they made, and the connections they found to their own lives and extend those reflective ideas to their own narratives. A sample prompt might read:

> At the beginning of this unit, you were asked to consider who you are, the ways you believe your identity to be fluid, and how understanding more about yourself and your relationship to others impacts your own development. You then used a range of activities to analyze the journeys of self-discovery of the major characters (e.g., Danny, Uno) in *Mexican Whiteboy*. Now that you have wrestled with identity and self-discovery throughout this unit, your next task is to take those experiences and apply them to yourself—to your own narrative of self-discovery.

In this narrative of approximately four to six pages, students will respond to the following guiding question: In what ways have you come to better understand yourself throughout this unit? Stated another way, describe the ways this unit has helped you to set off on your own journey of self-discovery. In yet other words, tell your own story of growth and development over the past five weeks.

To complete the assignment, students will draw on their reflective journal entries, class discussions, and analytical reading of the text. These will serve as the fuel that drives their composing. Note also that, while students may reference anything from your journals, notes, and experiences, the focus of this writing should be *them* and *their* journeys of self-discovery.

UNIT MATERIALS INVENTORY

Anchor Text:

de la Peña, Matt. *Mexican Whiteboy*. New York, NY: Delacorte Press, 2008.
Short Stories:
Birthday Box, a short story by Jane Yolen
Desiree's Baby, a short story by Kate Chopin

Poetry:

Endless Search by Alonzo Lopez. Retrieved January 28, 2020, from http://www.uram amurthy.com/gems/gem95.html

I, Too by Langston Hughes. Retrieved January 28, 2020, from https://www.poetryfo undation.org/poems/47558/i-too

Poem Full of Worry Ending with My Birth by Tarfia Faizullah. Originally published in Poem-a-Day on April 10, 2018, by the Academy of American Poets. Retrieved February 18, 2020 https://poets.org/poem/poem-full-worry-ending-my-birth

Nonfiction:

Pyrillis, R. (April 24, 2004). Sorry for not being a stereotype. *The Chicago Sun-Times*. Retrieved February 20, 2020, from http://libwww.freelibrary.org/onebook/obop11/0_Absolutely_True_Diary_Curriculum _full.pdf

Understanding Strangers from *Stories of Identity* (pp. 10-14)

Songs:

I'm Not a Girl (Not Yet a Woman), recorded by Britney Spears
Try It on My Own, recorded by Whitney Houston
Gravity, recorded by Alison Krauss
Coming of Age, recorded by Memphis Bleek
A Hero Lies in You, recorded by Mariah Carey
Holding Out for a Hero, recorded by Bonnie Tyler

YouTube Videos:

Adichie, C. N. (2009). The danger of a single story. TEDGlobal. Retrieved March 21, 2020, from https://www.ted.com/talks/chimamanda_ngozi_adichie_the_dange r_of_a_single_story

"I am sorry for not being the Stereotype" by Ingrid Marsh Retrieved March 21, 2020, https://www.youtube.com/watch?v=8cCCEtvNayM

Mexican Whiteboy - book trailer https://www.youtube.com/watch?v=uL2Gzjxr334

de la Peña, M. *We Need Diverse Books*. Retrieved March 18, 2020, https://www.ind iegogo.com/projects/we-need-diverse-books#/

Table 3.8 Additional Resources for Teachers

Fiction
Salinger, J. D. (1991). *The Catcher in the Rye*. Little, Brown And Company.
Myers, W. D. (1999). *Monster*. Harper Collins Publishers.
Chbosky, S. (1999). *The Perks of Being a Wallflower*. Pocket Books.
Green, J. (2005). *Looking for Alaska*. Dutton Children's.
Yang, G. L. (2006). *American Born Chinese*. First Second.
Nonfiction
Erikson, E. (1968). *Identity: Youth and Crisis*. W. W. Norton & Company, Inc.
Kroger, J. (2004). *Identity in Adolescence: The Balance Between Self and Other*. Routledge.
Quinn-Sanchez, K. (2015). *Identity in Latin American and Latina Literature: The Struggle to Self-Define In a Global Era Where Space, Capitalism, and Power Rule*. Lexington Books.
Media and Web Resources
King, R. C. What's the Hardest Part of Being a Teen? Retrieved March 9, 2020, http://wnpr.org/post/what-s-hardest-part-about-being-teen.
Vellekamp, L. Being a Teen. TED Talk. YouTube.com. June 3, 2016. Accessed March 4, 2020. https://youtu.be/L2iqczxkB-s.
Willis, J., M.D. What to Do About Your Teenager's Eye-Roll. Retrieved March 9, 2020, https://www.psychologytoday.com/blog/radical-teaching/201305/what-do-about-your-teenager-s-eye-roll

ADDITIONAL RESOURCES FOR TEACHERS

The unit material inventory provided in the previous section consists of the anchor text, *Mexican Whiteboy*, and other supplemental materials to examine the overarching theme of self-discovery using the main text. Teachers may develop similar units exploring other young adult novels. Table 3.8 presents other possible novels that may become focal in examining identity development issues, additional nonfiction and media texts to support these studies.

KEY ELEMENTS OF THE INSTRUCTIONAL UNIT

This chapter introduces a conceptual teaching unit focused on a journey of self-discovery. Readers will find helpful suggestions including:

- Rationale justifying the need for this unit and its brief overview;
- Overarching concepts, essential questions, and unit objectives, which will guide students' learning throughout the unit;
- A calendar plan presenting a unit at a glance with major activities, strategies, and assignments;
- Examples of possible activities connected to the thematic exploration of the novel and self-discovery and leading to the culminating narrative writing project;

- A list identifying anchor text and supplemental materials for the suggested unit of study;
- Additional resources to explore the theme of self-discovery.

Teachers and teacher educators may use this unit example as a working model for developing their own instructional sequence and materials.

Chapter 4

Good versus Bad, Right versus Wrong, and Other Choices

THEMATIC CONTEXT AND TRADITIONAL APPROACHES

From the moment children come into this life, they are introduced to the concepts of good and bad, right and wrong, and they are encouraged to make good choices. At first, parents, grandparents, other relatives, neighborhood and community members, and later teachers, coaches, counselors, and others shape children's attitudes, worldviews, and actions in response to their surroundings. Every time children respond to life events, they are making a decision and dealing with choices. At times, it seems the choices are extremely difficult, and no one wins the case at hand.

Too often adolescents face challenges that require immediate responses or actions. They ask themselves a myriad of questions on a daily basis: Should I wear jeans or a skirt today? Will my classmates mock my outfit? Do I help a friend who is "drowning" during the test? Should I stand up for an ostracized kid? Isn't it easier to mind my own business all the time? Some questions are easy to resolve, meanwhile others require more thought, assistance, and even courage to find the answer.

Because children spend much of their lives at school, teachers may provide needed support and assist students in navigating this world, in which every step requires thoughtful decision making. English teachers have obvious advantages simply because the battle between good and bad is a timeless universal theme in literature. Whether it is a myth, legend, folk tale, short story, novel, or someone's biography, the characters are involved in situations requiring an adequate action or reaction based on understanding of what is right, good, or best under the circumstances.

It is crucial to remember that these dichotomous concepts have never been constant: they are changing, that is, what was considered good centuries ago may not be valued as such today. Moreover, people's understanding of what is good or bad, or right and wrong, depends on their cultural, religious, economic, and educational contexts, and even on their familial values. When one of the context variables changes, there is a shift in the meaning of an entire specific concept.

Historians claim that the concept of good and evil is rooted in the religious insights of the Persian philosopher Zoroaster (or Zarathustra). He reveals his idea of a celestial struggle between Ahura Mazda, a *God of Wisdom and Good*, and Angra Mainyu, a *Destructive Spirit*. People on Earth support the ancient Gods' fight by taking sides. According to Zoroaster, living a virtuous life contributes to the triumph of good over evil (Violatti, 2019, para 11). Further, these ideas find sustenance in Chinese, Greek, and Roman mythologies, in religious books, oral traditions of every culture, and these concepts are generously employed in literary texts.

In fact, it is almost impossible to find a literary text that does not deal with the theme of Good versus Bad or Right versus Wrong. Literary characters fight their battles on one side or another, and occasionally find themselves in the crossroads, tangled in a clash of both sides manifesting their internal struggles. Along with literary characters, teachers and students may ponder critical life questions, discuss and evaluate characters' choices while thinking about similar experiences and drawing connections.

For decades, English teachers have been bringing famous canonic texts to explore this universal theme. Some use *The Iliad, The Odyssey*, or *Beowulf*, discussed in chapter 2, and others turn to *The Tragical History of the Life and Death of Doctor Faustus*, commonly referred to simply as *Doctor Faustus*, an Elizabethan tragedy by Christopher Marlowe. Yet, there is a great number of teachers favoring Shakespeare's tragedies, such as *King Lear, Hamlet, Prince of Denmark*, or *Macbeth*. These literary texts often feature characters who may begin their journeys on the "good" side, but their path is altered toward bad or evil under the influence of other people, circumstances, and/or choices.

Good versus Bad in Children's Stories, Fairy Tales, and Mythology

Most of the time, the good or bad decisions characters make in the above mentioned texts lead readers, including high school students, to easily label them as "good" or "bad" characters, and their choices as "right" or "wrong." In real life, the situation is more complex: sometimes good people make wrong decisions, and other times they do not have enough courage to choose what is right or to ask for help to avoid mistakes. The line between good and bad or right and wrong seems more intricate and blurred for contemporary young people.

Take, for example, children's stories or fairy tales many have experienced reading or listening to at some point. It seems right to blame a wolf for hunting down a little lamb from a famous *The Wolf and the Lamb* children's story calling the wolf cunning, greedy, and wicked. When the story is read and discussed with young children, there is not much exploration into the wolf's life or background, as there is no attempt to understand what drives the wolf's actions. Parents and teachers most likely explain to children that they shouldn't be like the wolf; instead, they have to be kind and helpful to others, but it might be easier and more effective to teach children with more realistic characters with which they can associate themselves.

Another traditional way of teaching the theme of Good versus Bad or Right versus Wrong is to introduce students, often beginning in middle grades, to Greek or Roman mythology. Mythology represents one of the richest heritages of ancient Greece and Rome, including myths of origin and creation, heroic myths, as well as the stories that educate about cultural, religious, and human values of the ancient world. Mythology is a precious gift from the past to the future with innumerable lessons.

As rich, amazing, and intriguing as myths and legends are, there is an immense gap between contemporary cultures that can be overwhelming to the present generation of high school students. They need to see the relevance and be able to draw connections, so learning about ancient heroes and their choices does not become another compilation of knowledge without real-life attachment and implications. Adolescents today live in a different society with different social, cultural, economic, gender, educational, and other norms. They are far removed from the experiences ancient societies treated as acceptable.

For example, it was common for early societies that women were often considered as objects of property, slavery was in place, no one questioning human rights, and many social and power struggles were resolved through violence (Hiatt, 2019). Moreover, lying, betraying, and killing "enemies" were thought to be unquestionably honorable. Is it acceptable today? Does reaching an end goal justify means undertaken to achieve it? What does it mean to be honorable, proud, and goal-oriented today? These are some of the questions ancient mythology is unable to address without additional and/or intentional effort.

To explore mythology further, we may notice numerous inconsistencies because these stories came to us through the writings of authors over the span of not only decades but centuries. So, for example, "Hesiod describes Cronus as imprisoned in Tartarus in one work but says he was ruling Elysium in another" (Hiatt, 2019, para 2). The cultural discrepancies with which students struggle while reading and responding to mythological stories, those that may interest mythology scholars and researchers, can create more frustration and confusion in teen readers.

Finally, contradictions in myths occur not only in the way that the story is told or events recounted but also in characters' behaviors. Many mythological characters are not relatable to students because they are incredibly unpredictable. It is one thing when a real person, who usually acts one way, makes a mistake and changes behavior or reacts to something differently once. In this case, after realizing the mistake this person may go back to old ways and self-correct. As humans, we make choices, and sometimes these choices are not right. The situation is a little different with Gods and their stories.

For example, reading myths involving Aphrodite, the Greek Goddess of love and beauty and marriage patron, there is evidence that beyond her role as gentle patron of love, she has a dark side. On the one hand, she pities Pygmalion and brings to life a statue of a woman he carved and subsequently fell in love with. On the other, she herself has affairs with most of the Olympian Gods and two mortals, having several children from different men. Yet, in other stories, she appears wrathful and unforgiving as she destroys the lives of Hippolytus, Eos, Diomedes, and Psyche (Hamilton, 1969).

To sum up, cultural gaps, inconsistencies in telling of the myths, and unrelatable, unpredictable characters are not the best fit for teenagers and their struggle and inquiry to accept and understand complex concepts as they relate to their personal experiences. There has to be a purposeful approach and efforts to make stronger connections when studying mythology, or teachers should consider introducing other kinds of stories to discuss right or wrong choices and good or bad actions. These stories have to present contemporary adolescents with realistic characters who face and struggle with challenges that are relevant today. Yet, over and over again, teachers turn to classic texts.

Shakespearean Tragedies as Mentor Texts in the Classroom

In high school, students often read one of Shakespeare's tragedies aiming to determine themes of Good versus Bad or Right versus Wrong. The most often taught are *Julius Caesar*, *Hamlet*, and *Macbeth*. At the core of each of these tragedies are the characters' actions driving the conflicts and resulting in evil choices. In each of the plays, there is a battle between good and evil, whether internal or external. Again, these battles and choices are not overly complicated to identify and evaluate.

For example, in *Hamlet* (Shakespeare, 1599–1609), a young Prince Hamlet is grieving the loss of his father and later learns that his father was murdered. A ghost of his father seeks revenge, and as a result, Hamlet steps on the road of evil and kills several people. Finally, he completes his goal and kills his father's murderer, his Uncle Claudius. For readers it may seem that seeking revenge is a noble cause; however, Hamlet's pursuit of it raises his internal struggles deciding whether he should kill the others or himself. He is destroyed as a result, losing peace of mind and eventually his life. It is obvious from this tragedy that righteousness does not always prevail.

As great as Shakespeare's tragedy is, it is over 400 years old. Life, as contemporary young adults know it, is inevitably different; the societal order has changed drastically, and the moral choices today are also significantly different from those of Hamlet's. The issues of throne inheritance, royal pride and honor, together with a necessity to defend them ceased to exist in much of the contemporary world. Even countries that preserved some form of a monarchy are governed by civil and criminal laws unlike the medieval Western world.

Many adolescents find Shakespeare unappealing, dreadful, and boring despite his immense contribution to world literature. As Cramer (2016) suggests, today it is about the way teachers present the bard to students. It "is important to hand adolescents versions of Shakespeare's plays that they can connect to, ones that provide a variety of ways to scaffold and support independent readers. Without these, any teen would groan and curse his name." Further, Cramer suggests innovative versions of Shakespearian texts and YA novels that may engage and sustain students' interest in Shakespeare's timeless stories of good and bad, love, life and death, friendship, and betrayal. Teachers may just need to find the right books to put in the hands of adolescents.

While the concepts of good and bad are timeless, and people were, are, and will always face a need to make choices based on their beliefs and moral values, the classic texts and their characters' experiences are considerably distanced from the current generation of high school students. With few exceptions, teenagers today live in a society where technology is pervasive in all spheres of life, and who is a breadwinner in the family does not matter for many cultures. That said, the ubiquitous nature of technology does not guarantee that all students have equitable access. The 2020 COVID-19 pandemic, for example, revealed huge inequity in terms of technology accessibility for many families with school-age children across the country, from urban to rural areas.

It is also necessary to acknowledge that many students today live in nontraditional or nonnuclear families, a contextual variable that influences views on good and evil, right and wrong. Today, family make-ups and dynamics may represent unions that are non/traditional, bi/racial, bi/cultural, have different educational and religious backgrounds, and represent varying socioeconomic status and varying sexual orientations. When facing a difficult choice or making an important decision, today's adolescents approach the same situation differently. They take into account their immediate surroundings, peers and adults, school culture, and other factors. As a result, their response is individualized and based on their life experiences, on what is valued or rejected in their families or neighborhood communities, and on their personal understandings of the world.

This creates a case in favor of using contemporary realistic fiction and nonfiction that more closely reflect adolescents and their lives in contemporary society considering an array of social, political, cultural, and moral issues present in society. Seeing themselves in the literature allows them to draw connections and recognize their struggles. Teachers understand that, in addition to mastering academic skills, students learn to become active citizens and good people who take responsibility for their choices and are able to make thoughtful, effective decisions.

DRAWING CONNECTIONS TO STUDENTS' LIVES

In many school districts, the literary canon still dominates over teachers' choices, imposing the notion that it is every English teacher's hope and desire to see their students enjoying Homer and Shakespeare, Donne and Thackeray, Dickins and Hemingway, or Twain and Steinbeck. State Departments of Education, district leaders, and school administrators following the expectations of standards-driven teaching, learning, and assessments suggest that students should and will find engagement and interest in classic texts.

Agreeing that classic literature is, in some ways, timeless and carries important insights into human nature and social development from ancient times, many teachers, especially the younger generation, also realize that bringing these authors into the classroom causes the opposite effect. Too often, secondary school students lose interest in reading and become disengaged because teachers impose canonic texts employing almost a foreign language.

This happens because students, through no fault of their own, are not ready and have not been prepared to work with these texts. The lessons become more of arduous language acquisition exercises with looking up the words and constant reading of the explanatory notes. It seems like they have to "translate" the text to be able to understand it. No doubt, a few students, possibly two or three in class, might be interested in vocabulary explorations, but many are bored and lose connection to the text content. Besides, complicated "foreign" language and noticeable historic and cultural gaps do not make classic texts necessarily complex.

On the contrary, including contemporary YAL into the English classroom may prove to be more engaging and effective while also presenting works of high literary quality. Today's YA authors incorporate complex characters, subjects, and situations (Cart, 2010), which are more than stories about "who is dating whom" or "what happened to dad's car" (Kaplan & Olan, 2017). The range of issues and human dilemmas of contemporary adolescent experiences has been considerably increased in YA literature responding to societal, economic, cultural, racial, gender, and other vital problems society is facing.

This is not to say that this book suggests to replace all classic texts with young adult literature. There is room in the school curriculum to find the best way to integrate both. This volume offers teachers and students ideas for exploring adolescent characters who are at the center of diverse living and learning experiences (Salvner, 2001). Their stories illustrate for young readers what literature can be and how it helps build knowledge and perspectives that are relevant, timely, and crucial for understanding the world around them, embrace their identities, and make life choices that reflect students' values and experiences.

Teachers undoubtedly may use literary texts recommended by their school districts, or, if they have more flexibility, select other texts they consider more suitable for their student population. There are several YA titles for possible consideration at the end of chapter 5 of this book. For the purpose of this chapter, the young adult novel of choice is *All American Boys*, published in 2015 by Jason Reynolds and Brendan Kiely. The novel's primary thematic focus unfolds around making difficult choices in a racially divided society. The main characters have to decide what is right or wrong and how to react in response to the situation in which they find themselves.

In the section that follows, readers will find a brief summary of *All American Boys*, connected to the themes of Good versus Bad, Right versus Wrong, and making choices. This novel will be an anchor text for an instructional unit, presented as an example for teachers to consider in chapter 5.

NOVEL OVERVIEW: *ALL AMERICAN BOYS* BY JASON REYNOLDS AND BRENDAN KIELY (2015)

Written by Jason Reynolds and Brendan Kiely, *All American Boys* (2015) is a Coretta Scott King Books Award novel featuring two young adult protagonists. Rashad Butler and Quinn Collins tell the story alternating their perspectives. The two young men live seemingly normal lives of high school students until they find themselves in an extreme situation. Rashad is the victim of a senseless and horrific beating at the hands of a cop and wakes up in a hospital, while Quinn, along with a camera, witnesses the event unfold.

To complicate the situation, Rashad Butler is Black, and Quinn Collins is White. Both sixteen-year-old boys face hard choices while grappling with the complications of brutal violence. Rashad struggles to accept his role as a victim of police brutality and join his voice with the school and community's response to racial hostility. Quinn has to decide his place in a deeply divided community. He has to wrestle with his whiteness and how that does or does not influence his perception and reaction. What makes the decision even harder is the fact that the cop, who brutally beats an innocent teenager, is Quinn's close family friend and his best friend's big brother.

The novel raises issues of personal growth through trauma, racism and social justice, community identity, and adolescent activism. It prompts readers to follow the characters who are forced to grow up fast, determine what is right, define what is wrong, make difficult choices, and take sides. The novel's finale promises hope for tomorrow, in which people can come together to solve problems and work together to provide support and interrupt racism and inequity.

YAL AND THEMATIC EXPLORATION: *ALL AMERICAN BOYS* AND DIFFICULT CHOICES

This section provides a detailed thematic analysis of the chapter to serve as an example for teachers. Too often thematic discussions in class turn into mere naming the important topics or universal themes and lack a substantial, close examination of how the theme is developed and what readers actually learn from the novel about these universal themes.

In *All American Boys* (2015), Reynolds and Kiely tell a story that is all too familiar and painfully real to anyone living in the United States today. Readers may identify several major issues the novel presents and carefully explores employing two adolescent narrators, Rashad Butler and Quinn Collins. Among these are relevant issues related to racism and police brutality targeting young representatives of a marginalized population. However, the act of unjust police violence has happened at the very beginning of the novel, and from that moment, the central focus shifts to the societal response in connection with it.

The characters have to make choices, decide what is right or wrong, and defend their decisions and the subsequent actions they take. Thus the novel becomes about difficult choices which lead to a huge positive step toward the triumph of good over evil (i.e., systemic racism) in the community surrounding the protagonists. Each choice is associated with certain risks and raises additional questions:

- Is it worth standing up for myself?
- What is better: staying loyal to friends and family or doing the right thing?
- Who decides what is wrong and what is right?

- Why do people have to make choices if sometimes these choices distance them from their loved ones or friends?

Readers witness that, from the very beginning of the novel, Rashad Butler is facing choices. Some choices are trivial and non-essential: what shirt to wear or what snack to choose. When Rashad walks into Jerry's store, for example, and sees "the stank-breath flavors" of chips, he tries to find one "most easily beaten by a stick of gum" (Reynolds & Kiely, p. 18) because he plans to meet with a girl he likes and wants to enjoy a Friday night party.

There are other cases though, in which Rashad does not have much choice, like with joining ROTC. "I didn't want to be a part of no military club," he points out and insists: "I didn't need ROTC. But I did it, and did it good, because my dad was pretty much making me" (Reynolds & Kiely, p.6). As an African American, Mr. Butler believes that his son would be safer and better off in the military since "there's no better opportunity for a black boy in this country than to join the army" (p. 6). The army, he believes, may provide a less racially charged environment unlike any civil career. Subconsciously, the young man understands his dad's intentions and complies.

The events develop rapidly, and choices become crucial when a lady trips over Rashad in a neighborhood store. A store assistant immediately blames the boy for "trying to steal those chips" (p. 21) and a cop, who happens to be in the store, shoves him through the door and slams him to the ground. The cop, Officer Paul Galluzzo, does not waste time and does not try to find out what has happened. He mercilessly beats up Rashad, breaking the boy's nose and hurting him everywhere he could reach with his feet and fists while blaming him for resisting arrest.

Avoiding the officer's hits, Rashad moves, and it costs him an even worse round of pounding. He doesn't want to resist. His only thoughts at that moment are: "I didn't want to resist . . . I just wanted to stop him beating me. I just wanted to live" (Reynolds & Kiely, p.23). The young man does live but finds himself in a hospital "with a broken nose and a few fractured ribs" (p. 43) drifting in and out of sleep induced by painkillers.

It is important to note that the store clerk and the officer also make choices in this situation. The first one looks at Rashad suspiciously from the moment the boy enters the store. It seems the guy is always on the lookout for people like Rashad Butler, so his choice to instantaneously blame the young man for stealing is predetermined and not complicated by additional thought or willingness to find out what is really happening.

The second one, the officer, seems concerned at first, but his concern is about the lady who tripped. He does not even let her complete a sentence explaining that she lost her balance. Galluzzo jumps at Rashad seeing him as a thug, who needs "to learn how to respect authority" (p. 23). Later, Paul

Galluzzo maintains the position justifying his choice by insisting that he is just doing his job. How does beating up a teenage boy in cuffs, breaking his nose and ribs qualify for anyone's job description? This remains an open question for multiple witnesses of the scene.

The horrific beating happens during the day with people on the street watching; some are trying to say: "Leave him alone," and someone is video-recording the entire incident. Among those watching is Quinn Collins, a high school senior, "the All-American boy with an All-American fifteen-foot deadeye jump shot and an All-American 3.5 GPA" (p. 27). He, too, sees a Black boy around his age, looking "vaguely familiar" (p.34) being beaten by a White cop. When he recognizes Paul—his best friend's older brother—as the cop, he is bewildered, "sorta frozen, just watching, transfixed" (Reynolds & Kiely, p. 34).

Quinn's first decision is to run away from the scene and stay away from police business. He knows though that there is something utterly wrong with Paul's behavior. Quinn Collins keeps thinking about the witnessed incident, but is unable to shake off "that look of rage" in a man, who is almost an older brother to him after his dad died in Afghanistan. This young man has to make a tough decision: stay loyal to a family friend and his best friends or confront them and do the right thing.

The decision is the most difficult one Quinn has ever made. He feels pressure from Guzzo's family, from his classmates who are on Paul's side, and from his mother who is afraid her son will suffer by getting caught up in this racial conflict. She wants to protect her son the only way she can, by removing him from the events; however, she understands how crucial the right choice is for everyone in the community.

Eventually, Quinn makes desperately brave choices. First, he calls the police to make a statement and then decides to join a march organized by Rashad's friends and classmates involving most of their high school. These are not easy decisions for Quinn; they come with a toll of being rejected by close friends and with possible prosecution by city and police officials for attending an unauthorized public "event." Truly understanding the meaning of one of the quotes from Desmond Tutu: "If you are neutral in situations of injustice, you have chosen the side of the oppressor" (Reynolds & Kiely, p. 290); he is glad to follow his conscience.

Meanwhile, recovering in the hospital after the horrific beating, Rashad feels overwhelmed by all the attention drawn to the incident by the media. It seems too much and too painful for him to handle. He admits that he "didn't want to hear Spoony preach about how hard it is to be black, or my father preach about how young people lack pride and integrity, making us easy targets" (Reynolds & Kiely, p. 101). However, his brother, Spoony, and conversations about the civil rights movement with Shirley Fitzgerald convince him to stand up for justice. At the end of the novel, he embraces his role as an agent of change for African American people affected by police brutality.

From the point of joining the march, both Rashad and Quinn are "present" in the moment. They both realize that their ultimate choices are important; they are worth any risks because, as Rashad concludes, they are "for all the people who came before us, fighting this fight" (p. 310). For these seventeen-year-olds, a wake-up call happens early allowing them to be the best versions of themselves.

Presented here is a possible way for teachers to lead their students through explorations of the main characters and their choices. The novel also presents several minor characters whose thoughts and actions add to the theme of facing difficult choices. Examining the protagonists' friends, parents, and media representation adds to the depth and range of the thematic interpretations. To analyze the theme development, teachers may engage students in small and whole-class discussions around characters, events, and settings.

KEY IDEAS

This chapter introduces the theme of making choices between good and bad or right and wrong. First, it establishes the origins of the concept of good and evil. Further, it examines ways the theme has often been taught in the English classroom, which is mostly through short stories, fairy tales and mythology in elementary and middle schools, and through Shakespearean plays in high school.

Next, the chapter discusses how the theme of good versus bad can be explored by contemporary adolescents through making difficult choices or choosing right versus wrong. This section also advocates in favor of using young adult literature that is relevant to students and their lived experiences.

Finally, the chapter provides a brief summary of *All American Boys* (Reynolds & Kiely, 2015) as a method for engaging students in theme analysis. As an example for teachers, the chapter offers a useful starting point for students' explorations based on the novel's two major characters and choices they have to make.

The following chapter presents readers with an outline of an instructional unit using *All American Boys* as an anchor text to conduct a thorough investigation into difficult decisions the characters are forced to make. The suggested unit will present opportunities to connect the novel examination with the lives and experiences of the students in the classroom.

Chapter 5

Conceptual Teaching Unit

Examination of Good versus Bad, Right versus Wrong, and Other Choices

The sample teaching unit provided in this chapter is centered around the themes of Good versus Bad, Right versus Wrong, and making challenging choices. This specific instructional sequence is developed for high school students and may fit into the eleventh or twelfth grade English curriculum. In fact though, this is an ongoing theme relevant to any classroom because it helps develop moral values and teaches making decisions that are not often easy.

In elementary school, teachers and parents explain to their children the importance of being polite, kind to each other, and sharing toys, snacks, or room. The children may learn from fairy tales, short stories, and children's rhymes. In the following middle school years, students may focus on issues of honesty or bullying within this theme. Middle schoolers are inquisitive and aware and are capable of understanding societal issues, such as inequity or racism, if the learning is scaffolded and progresses to build up their knowledge and develop a critical approach throughout readings, discussions, and activities.

By the time teenage students are in high school, teachers are actively preparing them for an adult world in which one of the most valuable qualities becomes integrity, unifying and strengthening everything that was taught earlier—compassion, honesty, high moral principles and beliefs, and so on. The world students inhabit and will enter more fully after schooling requires regular responses, based on individual beliefs and values, to events, conditions, and situations. This world requires choices that are difficult, unpredictable, and often convoluted, but that are inevitable and important.

The suggested unit is planned for approximately four weeks of study in the classroom; however, these are not strict guidelines, and teachers may extend it up to two more weeks. The extended unit will work well in case teachers include more supplementary readings and culminating writing projects that require students to spend additional time conducting research and sharpening writing skills. Placing this instructional sequence after the unit on self-discovery (described in chapter 3) may prove to be beneficial.

As part of figuring out who they are, young people also strive to understand what makes them better and how to become their best selves. In this regard, the unit continues the conversation about self-discovery and self-construction. The ability to differentiate between right and wrong and an ability to make a thoughtful decision will assist them to be more confident and self-reliant. Even further, the decisions and actions students undertake help them to form their future selves. In addition, by thinking and learning about challenging choices, students will be able to better understand what it means to be self-content and to have integrity.

Furthermore, charged with critical response to societal issues, this unit would fit well either as one before winter break, possibly the third unit of the fall semester, or the first unit of the spring semester in January. Teachers and students will have time to learn about each other and form trustworthy relationships, which will help when discussing sensitive topics requiring honest responses and allowing students to take a social position based on their beliefs and values.

Finally, placing the unit in the middle or second half of the school year may also prove helpful as students move from personal narrative expressions and writing toward more academic discussions and formal writing of an argumentative nature with strong textual support. They will learn about developing research questions, and conducting research necessary to support claims based on literary analysis, which include devoting time to citing, the use of direct and indirect quotes, and formatting requirements.

The unit described in this chapter builds on the discussion of a young adult text in chapter 4. A wide variety of young adult texts would be appropriate for thematic explorations of good, bad, right, wrong, and other choices. This conceptual teaching unit is built around *All American Boys*, written by J. Reynolds and B. Kiely in 2015. The events in the novel are recognizable and relevant to students' lives and reflect societal struggles today. The story addresses racial, cultural, and socioeconomic diversities, which are all present in and relevant to public schools.

Similar to the previous unit, described in chapter 3, this sequence and its anchor novel allow for activities and discussions that strongly support anti-racism. As educators, it is imperative to teach students to identify and actively confront and challenge racism in all of its obvious and hidden forms. Creating a safe space for students to bring their concerns about the outside world into the classroom will provide opportunities for embracing reality, facilitating difficult conversations, and most importantly, giving students a voice.

To supplement the theme exploration, students will also read, think, and discuss poetry, three short stories, and view YouTube videos. These additional materials are listed in the *Unit Materials Inventory* section of this chapter. The goal is to expose students to multimodal varieties of texts, which are in print, nonprint, digital, and art forms.

In-class and homework activities and projects for this unit address all the texts throughout the unit. They are constructed with the goal of building students' understanding of the concepts of choice and responsibilities for decisions they make. Students are assigned homework reading of the novel *All American Boys* during the first two weeks. They will keep a *Dialogue Journal* throughout this time to record their questions, quotes, and interpretation of selected passages from the novel. Daily novel discussions will result in a *Socratic Seminar* to solidify students' understanding of the novel and theme explorations.

Moreover, students are offered opportunities to complete several mini-creative projects: *Character Mind Map*, *Graffiti Activity*, and *Second Chance*, which will be explained later in this chapter. The post-assessment consists of a final unit test and a thematic analysis essay in the form of an argument. The first part of it is a combined multiple-choice and short constructed-response test based on the unit readings and in-class activities. For the second part, students have to develop their paper considering the anchor novel, poems, short stories, and nonfiction pieces they read throughout the unit, as well as two or three outside scholarly sources to support their claims.

The ongoing and final academic tasks will provide teachers with an evaluation of students' understanding of the overarching unit concepts and achieving the unit objectives. They will also assess students' abilities to conduct thematic analysis and present a literary argument, along with their reading, writing, and critical thinking performance.

OVERARCHING CONCEPTS, ESSENTIAL QUESTIONS, AND UNIT OBJECTIVES

Continuing to prepare high schoolers to navigate in real-world spaces, including college and their future work careers, this unit will focus around the concepts of good and bad, right, and wrong as it relates to choices they make daily. Thus, using *All American Boys* (Reynolds & Kiely, 2015) as an anchor literary text and employing a variety of supplemental multimodal texts, this teaching sequence allows students to utilize literary analysis as a method to scrutinize and further explore themselves and their decision-making practices.

This unit relies on students' previous knowledge of the concepts of good and bad, right and wrong by taking it to a personal level complicated with current societal struggles with norms and accepted views. In elementary and middle schools, students read and analyzed various literary texts, including, but not limited to short stories, fairy tales, Greek or Roman mythology, Shakespearean plays, and/or novels, in which characters made choices and faced challenges requiring determination and courage. Because a YA novel with adolescent characters is at the center of this unit, it will be more relatable and engaging for high school students.

Engaging with a novel such as *All American Boys* (Reynolds & Kiely, 2015) around these critical concepts creates opportunities for students to (1) advance their skills in literary analysis and writing about it and (2) become active agents of change applying the concepts of good and bad, right and wrong to make choices crucial to society's struggles for social equality and justice.

The proposed emphasis on integrity, facing challenges, and responsibility for made decisions, this unit becomes relevant and individualized for every student in the classroom. Understanding that students entering the English classroom are from different families, have diverse cultural, economic, and educational backgrounds, as well as various religious and personal moral values, the teacher's major role is to embrace and welcome multiplicity of perspectives enriching learning experiences.

Reading about the events described in the novel, students will be able to relate to its characters and their actions, recognizing the social issues that society is facing and needs to resolve. They will be able to identify and analyze choices that these characters make and evaluate them based on individual understanding. Throughout the unit, students, with the teacher's guidance, will grapple with the following questions:

- What is considered good or bad in our society? Is it the same for all the groups within the society?
- Who decides what is good or bad?
- How do we know if a choice is wrong?
- What does it mean to be a person of integrity?
- Why does making a choice become an individual responsibility?
- How does an individual choice affect people around us?

Since the suggested unit serves as a model, there might be an opening for other questions in connection with the thematic exploration. Some questions may arise from a specific region or make up of the class in which this unit is taught. Teachers are welcome to include what they consider vital to ponder and discuss throughout this instructional sequence.

Along with critical thinking about the overarching concepts and essential questions, students will be able to enhance their academic analytical and writing skills. By the end of the unit, students should be able to:

- read and understand complex texts;
- cite relevant textual evidence that supports literary analysis;
- identify one or more themes in literary works;
- analyze theme development through point of view, settings, and plot;
- analyze how complex characters develop over the course of a text;
- compose well-developed constructed responses to texts;
- develop argumentative writing based on literary analysis;
- conduct research to support an argument;
- apply the steps of the writing process to compose writing for a given task;
- write routinely in response to texts and class discussions;
- participate in a variety of collaborative activities;
- understand academic vocabulary;
- apply MLA/APA formatting style to academic writing; and
- demonstrate command of language conventions when writing.

The following section introduces a sample of a calendar plan for a teaching unit focused on the concepts of good and bad, right and wrong, and making choices. Teachers may use it in its entirety or choose instructional strategies, activities, and assessments that will be effective in their classrooms.

CALENDAR PLAN FOR A CONCEPTUAL TEACHING UNIT

A calendar plan presenting a sample of the teaching unit at a glance is suggested below. Here teachers may see possible activities, projects, teaching strategies, assignments and homework to engage students in learning and thematic explorations based on the established overarching concepts, essential questions, and unit objectives. The unit is planned as a four-week study focusing on the concepts of Good versus Bad, Right versus Wrong, and on making difficult choices.

As with any new unit of study, it begins with a pre-assessment to evaluate what students already know about the theme and how they evaluate themselves and their decisions in relation to it. An introduction to the unit is implemented through a reflective journal, interactive video "Choices," and presentation of the unit theme and objectives. Building on prior knowledge, students advance their understanding of the major unit concepts through daily activities, projects, and writing tasks.

Focused around close reading of the anchor text, the unit materials are supplemented by a wide variety of other texts in print and nonprint form, including digital resources. Students' learning experiences involve collaborative, small, and whole-class activities as well as individual work to assess the progress of each student in the classroom. By the end of the unit, students will develop a literary-based argument to demonstrate their skills in literary analysis, writing, and understanding of the unit's concepts.

Tables 5.1–5.4 present an example of the calendar plan for four consecutive weeks of study centered around the theme of Good versus Bad, Right versus Wrong, and making challenging choices.

Week 1 introduces students to the unit theme and the variety of assignments they will be completing over the coming weeks. It begins with a reflective journal serving as pre-assessment aiming to evaluate students' prior knowledge, followed by a short video "Choices," featuring a high school student who's easily making various choices as he goes through the day until it gets more complicated. The goal of the first week is to announce the theme, unit of study with its major objectives and assignments, and the anchor text.

Table 5.1   Week 1

Day	Activities
Monday	Pre-assessment: Journal entry responding to the question: When did you have to make an important decision? Please share the moment and decision you made. How would you evaluate your decision today? "Choices"—an interactive short film (YouTube). Discuss Eleanor Roosevelt's introductory quote Introduction to the unit, its objectives, and major assignments

Tuesday	*Poetry Gallery Walk*: Poems about choices:
	   Dreams by L. Hughes
	   The Road Not Taken by Robert Frost
	   What is Success? by Ralph Waldo Emerson
	   Hard Choices by Jojoba Mansell
	Constructed response based on the *Poetry Gallery Walk*.

Wednesday	*Building Background Knowledge*: Jason Reynolds and Brendan Kiely Introducing the novel, *All American Boys* by Reynolds and Kiely Making inferences about the novel development Homework: read *Friday*, pp. 5–40 of the novel
Thursday	Analyzing the novel structure: Friday to Friday Reading and Discussing *All American Boys*: Friday events—establishing the context, setting, and characters. *Dialogue Journal* (will continue throughout the unit): recording quotes, questions, interpretations. Homework: Read *Saturday*, pp. 43–82
Friday	Reading and Discussing *All American Boys*: Authors' choices about narration—two points of perspective. Watching and analyzing animated scenarios. Developing vocabulary to analyze characters. Homework: Read *Sunday*, pp. 85–120 and *Monday*, pp. 123–162 Complete a *Dialogue Journal* with reading

Table 5.2 Week 2

Monday	Reading and discussing *All American Boys*: Major characters
	Interpretive discussions based on the *Dialogue Journal* (will continue throughout this week): quotes, questions, interpretations
	Homework: Read *Tuesday*, pp. 165–203
	Dialogue Journal
Tuesday	Reading and discussing *All American Boys*: the significance of the minor characters
	Creative mini-project: *Character Mind Map*
	Homework: Read *Wednesday*, pp. 207–246
	Dialogue Journal
Wednesday	Reading and discussing *All American Boys*: identifying themes and their development
	Theme Development Worksheet—Essential questions to consider
	Homework: Read *Thursday*, pp. 249–282
	Dialogue Journal
	Continue working on the *Character Mind Map*
Thursday	Reading and discussing *All American Boys*: pivotal moments in the main characters' and school community transformation
	Character Mind Map presentations and discussion
	Small-group work—*Graffiti Activity*
	Homework: Read *Friday*, pp. 285–310 (complete the novel reading)
	Dialogue Journal
Friday	Small-group work—*Graffiti Activity*—and presentation
	Connecting to classics: Reading and discussion of the short story *Good Country People* by Flannery O'Connor

Table 5.3 Week 3

Monday	Interview with the authors: YouTube video clips
	Socratic seminar introduction
	Literary analysis argumentative essay introduction
Tuesday	Connecting to classics: Reading and discussion of the short story *After Twenty Years* by O'Henry
	Developing questions for a Socratic seminar/Possible Research Questions
Wednesday	Connecting to world literature: Reading and discussion of the short story *Children of the Sea* by Edwidge Danticat
	Socratic seminar
Thursday	Preparing for writing: Elements and structure of an argument
	Read and discuss an excerpt from *Resistance to Civil Government* by Henry David Thoreau
Friday	Small-group work: *Second Chance* writing activity
	Research for supporting an argument: identifying quotes from the novel for the literary analysis essay

Table 5.4 Week 4

Monday	Reading and discussing *The Sit-In Movement* https://www.commonlit.org/en/texts/the-sit-in-movement
	Library or computer lab work: Research of scholarly articles to support an argument
Tuesday	Critical summary and evaluation of the sources
	Begin drafting of a literary analysis argumentative essay
Wednesday	Continue drafting of a literary analysis argumentative essay
	Teacher-student conferences to assist with drafting
Thursday	Peer review sessions with focus on content and structure of the argument
	Beginning of the revision process (if time permits)
Friday	Post-Assessment: final unit test
	The unit reflection
	Homework: Complete the final revisions and editing and prepare the essay for submission on Monday

Further, Week 1 leads to reading and discussion of the first half of the novel. The main instructional strategies and skills are centered on making inferences and keeping up dialog journals, in which students will record quotes that prompt their thinking and engagement with the novel, as well as questions and thoughts they have as they continue reading the novel. Friday's lesson will be devoted to an analysis of the narration and points of view in the novel. It will also help students develop a grade-appropriate vocabulary for character analysis.

Most of the Week 2 activities are suggested around reading and discussion of the novel. Students will continue *Dialog Journals* as they read the novel at home. The journal entries will help initiate class discussions. Students will closely analyze characters, identify major themes, and continue their exploration through *Character Mind Map* projects, theme development worksheet, and *Graffiti Activity*. The week will conclude with a *Graffiti Activity* presentation and reading a short story, *Good Country People* by Flannery O'Connor, to make a connection to classic literature.

Students will be able to identify the themes of the short stories and connect them to the themes of their anchor novel. They will be able to recognize story characters' choices, evaluate them, and make conclusions based on the concepts and understandings they formed throughout the first two weeks. Adapting this week's plan, teachers are welcome to include daily journals to begin each lesson, which may help initiate novel discussion and/or introduce an instructional strategy or activity.

Week 3 advances thematic explorations of the concepts of Good versus Bad, Right versus Wrong, and making difficult choices. This week's focus is on bridging classic short stories and an excerpt from *Resistance to Civil Government* by Henry David Thoreau with *All American Boys*, comparing the thematic messages, drawing connections, and determining differences in possible conflict resolutions. Socratic seminar and a small-group *Second Chance* writing activity aim to solidify students' understanding of the novel and character analysis, as well as students' personal position toward the social issues discussed in class.

Along with thematic discussions, students will be introduced to a culminating argumentative writing assignment based on literary analysis (Hillocks, 2011). They will review the elements of the argument, including its structure, and identify possible research questions, which could be built into a Socratic seminar discussion but need further investigation through research. Students will also reread parts of the novel more closely to identify quotes supporting their argument claims.

The fourth and final week of the unit is primarily devoted to argument writing. Students will work in the library or computer lab, if there are no laptops or other computer devices to work in the classroom, to conduct further research exploring the overarching concepts in scholarly publications. Teachers or librarians may plan a lesson on search engines, formatting style, summary, and critical evaluation of the sources, and other skills students may need for successful completion of the argumentative essay. This week will conclude with post-assessment and final unit reflection.

FOSTERING THEMATIC ANALYSIS OF GOOD VERSUS BAD, RIGHT VERSUS WRONG AND OTHER CHOICES: SAMPLE ACTIVITIES FOR ELA CLASSROOMS

In this section, teachers and educators will find examples of possible instructional activities, which they may use throughout the unit. Some activities are introductory and completed before reading the anchor text, while others follow the readings of the main novel and supplementary texts. Finally, there are enrichment activities that advance student learning and understanding of the thematic explorations to be completed after the reading of the novel.

It is helpful to remind that the discussion of each activity below includes an explanation of how to organize or conduct it, in addition to making connections to the anchor text and the instructional unit. Depending on students' identities, abilities, and learning backgrounds, along with available resources, teachers may modify activities to better suit their students and unit goals.

Introductory Activities

"Choices"—A Short Film Discussion

One of the activities leading to the unit introduction could be a screening of a short YouTube video, "Choices." It begins with the following quote by

Eleanor Roosevelt: "I am who I am today because of the choices I made yesterday." Teachers may use this quote for an opening discussion of the unit's theme. Students may share some of their past choices that may speak to how they view themselves presently. After a brief three to five minutes of discussion, the teacher and students continue watching the video.

This four-minute short film features a high school student, Mark, who is making choices throughout a regular day. Early in the morning he decides whether to wake up or go back to sleep, to put gel into his hair or not, to eat chocolate puffs or Special-K cereal for breakfast. As he gets to school, he makes other choices: to look stupid or ask for help during class work, to talk to a girl he likes or to pass by without even acknowledging her. All of the choices seem to come easy to him, except for the final, where the audience doesn't know Mark's answer. The film ends making us wonder whether Mark will ask a friend to get him a "good" pill for the party in the evening or not?

After the video, the teacher may lead into a discussion of the choice Mark may make, and students will infer possible outcomes of the situation. This activity may then transition to the formal introduction of the unit, its overarching concepts, objectives, and expectations for student achievements.

Poetry Gallery Walk

This is another introductory, or pre-reading, activity, which may set up the tone for thematic explorations. This discussion strategy allows students to be actively involved as they walk throughout the classroom. The teacher may break a class into groups of four or five students who work together to share ideas and respond to questions about the poems. There will be at least four Poetry Stations set up in the classroom. Each station will have a poem posted on the wall, which can be handwritten or typed and printed out in a larger font so each student can easily read.

Some of the poems that can be used for this gallery walk are: *Dreams* by Langston Hughes, *The Road Not Taken* by Robert Frost, *There Is a Difference* by William Henry Dawson, *Choices* by Nikki Giovanni, and *Hard Choices* by Jojoba Mansell. Each of the poems deals with choices and how people make them. Walking from one poetry station to another, each group of students will read a poem, identify its message and tone, and help them create their own definition of choice by the end of this activity.

Needless to say that teachers may offer other poems they know and prefer for this activity. While reading and discussing *All American Boys* and other literary texts, students will come back to their initial definition, revising and adding to it as they get a better understanding of the concepts at the core of the choice: Good versus Bad, Right versus Wrong.

Reading and Discussing the Novel

Dialog Journals

A dialogue journal presents a common practice of an informal written conversation between two or more people. It may happen between two students or between a student and a teacher. For this unit, each student in class is tasked with keeping up a dialogue journal during the first two weeks along with reading a novel. Students complete this as homework, but if there is only a class set of the novels, then teachers will allow about ten minutes of class time to complete the journal after reading the assigned pages.

For each of the assigned readings, students are to record up to three quotes they consider important to the understanding of the novel and overarching unit concepts and two or three questions they may have about the same reading. After that, students exchange their journal with assigned partners and respond to each other's comments and questions, thus having a conversation with each other about the novel, characters, their thoughts, actions, and choices.

Once or twice a week teachers may collect the journals, read through them, and also comment and respond to questions, turning it into a multivoice conversation. Another way to create a multivoice conversation is to change partners every two days, for example. This way, students in class will get several perspectives and feedback on their journal entries, and the teachers will not be overwhelmed by the weekly amount of reading and responding. Dialogue journals provide students with a meaningful writing activity that is engaging because it involves active interactions with peers. These written dialogues support learning while creating bonds between participating parties.

Character Mind Map

Character Mind Map is a visual representation of a literary character from the novel. Students may complete this project as a small group or individually. After announcing the project and deciding whether it is going to be a small-group or individual project, the teacher explains instructions and requirements of the project. To create a Character Mind Map, students have to choose a major or minor character from *All American Boys* and reflect the character's personal traits, thoughts, important choices, and how they lead to changes in this character and his/her environment (see table 5.5 for instructions).

Completing the project, students will be able to reflect on the character's choices, their understanding of right or wrong and good or bad. It will allow students to compare their own attitudes to similar experiences and possible choices they would make. After the presentations of the Character Mind Maps, the teacher may engage students in a follow-up whole-class discussion

Table 5.5 Character Mind Map

Character Mind Map

If you could look inside the character's head, what would we see?

You will be creating a mind map—a visual and written portrait illustrating a character's life within *All American Boys*.

Below, there are a few suggestions to complete the Character's Mind Map, but you are welcome to create your own vision of the chosen character. Keep in mind though that the choices you make should be based on the text. You will defend your choices in written form of about one page explaining why you designed the mind map the way you did. Think carefully about the choices you make; they have to be analytical, creative, and accurately based on the novel.

Mind Map Requirements

Although your mind map may contain additional dimensions, your portrait must contain:

- A character's name and title of the novel
- The character's personality traits and change in the work
- The character's thoughts and important choices
- Visual symbols
- The character's three most important quotes (or quotes describing the character)

Mind Map Suggestions

1. Values: What is the character's objective within a work? What is the most important goal for your character? What drives his/her thoughts and actions?
2. Strengths and Weaknesses: What are your character's most commendable qualities? What are the weak sides?
3. Color: Colors are often symbolic. What color(s) do you most associate with your character? Why? How can you integrate these colors into your visual map?
4. Symbols: Are there any objects illustrating the character's essence? If not, think of objects that may correspond with the character.
5. Conflicts and choices: What is the major struggle of the character? What choices does a character make? How do these choices affect the outcomes of the conflict?
6. Change: Has your character changed within the work? If yes, then how? What is the driving force for the change?

You may draw your own image or use a template with an image of a head from the Internet. While creativity is encouraged, the focus of the assignment is on your understanding, interpretation, and thoughts about the character in connection with the theme analysis.

---

which will advance understanding of the concepts of equality and equity in a racially divided society.

To complete the task, students carefully analyze the chosen character and compile information to support their analysis. That is why this activity is a direct contribution to the culminating argumentative essay based on a given character's choices. Below, readers can see an example of a Character Mind Map based on Rashad Butler. It reflects some of his thoughts, values, beliefs, fears, and choices (figure 5.1).

Examination of Good versus Bad, Right versus Wrong, and Other Choices 75

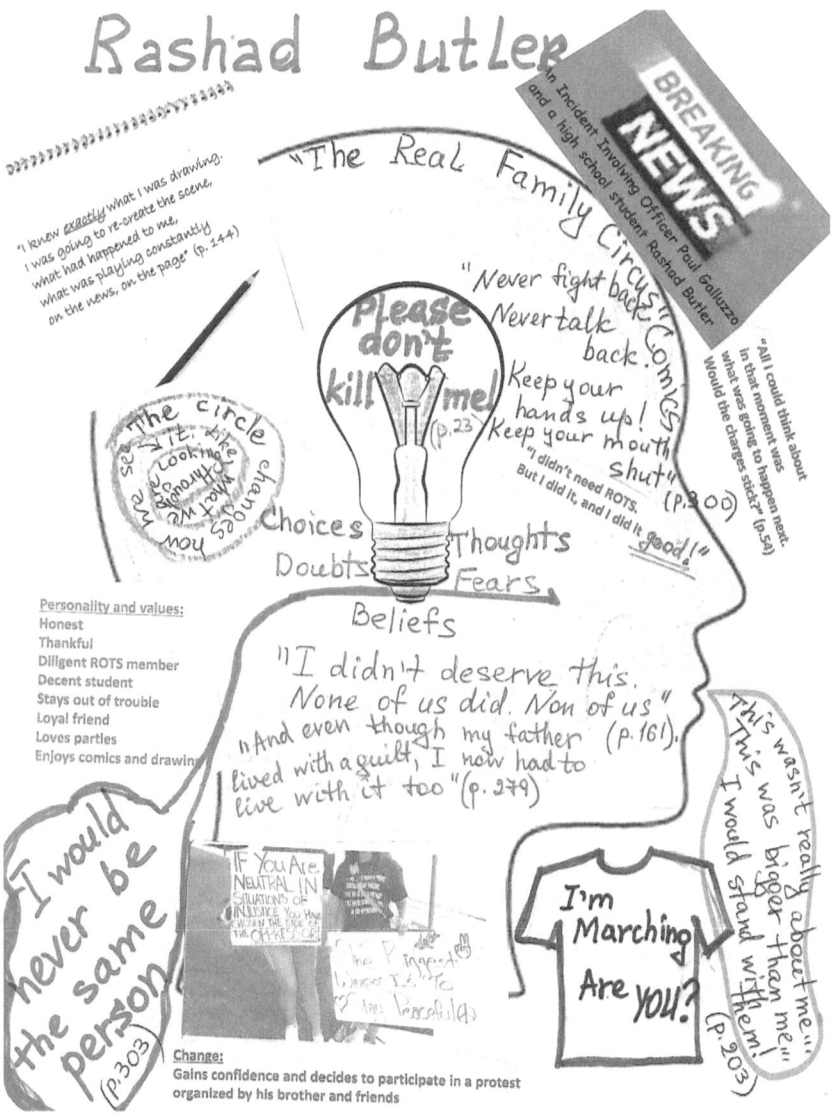

Figure 5.1 Rashad Butler, Character Mind Map. *Source*: Authors.

Graffiti Activity

In the novel Carlos, Rashad's friend, spray-paints a graffiti sign "Rashad Is Absent Again Today" (p. 165) on the sidewalk near the front stairs of the school entrance. It is huge, and seems that everyone has to step over or walk around it to get to the building. Later that night, social media is flooded with #RashadIsAbsentAgainToday. The slogan serves as a sad notice that Rashad has been robbed of education along with his other rights, highlighting the issue of how racism operates to limit the choices, educational opportunities, and success of minoritized and oppressed people.

Teachers may suggest students work in a group of four or five to create their own graffiti wall. A graffiti wall is a shared writing space where students record quotes, comments, and questions about a topic. The goal of this strategy is to help students "hear" and see each other's ideas. The strategy can be implemented in five to ten minutes or turned into a bigger project and completed in two sittings. Creating the graffiti wall provides a way for shy or quiet students to engage in class conversation. It also generates students' ideas and questions that can be used for later discussions, and it allows students space and time to process emotional material.

If there is enough space on the whiteboards in the classroom, teachers may use them for this activity. There are also smaller flexible whiteboards that might be available at school, but even regular poster paper will work. Before each group begins to work on its graffiti wall, the teacher explains the task and how to express one's discomfort with something in an appropriate way. After that, the teacher gives a specific task.

The group members are to choose a brief quote from *All American Boys* that reflects one of the characters' difficult choices and contributes to their understanding of the novel and concepts of right and wrong. They have to write the quote in the middle of their graffiti wall, whether it is a poster or whiteboard, and around the quote they have to write at least three comments explaining it. Students may also pose two to three questions for further discussion with their classmates. If teachers plan enough time for this activity, students may be creative and write the quote in graffiti style decorating the rest of the space as well (see figure 5.2).

After the project is complete, each of the groups presents it to class. The activity may be concluded with a whole-class discussion stemming from the quotes and questions that students generated in the graffiti walls. Teachers may take pictures of what the students create and publish them in the school's newspaper or bulletin. Depending on resources and teacher support, students could also collaborate to create a digital collage using all of the produced posters. This work could be later integrated into students' argumentative essays about choices, as there will be multiple quotes, comments, and questions for consideration.

Enrichment Activities

Second Chance Activity

To continue thinking about and exploring the theme of making choices and differentiating between right and wrong, teachers may include *Second*

Examination of Good versus Bad, Right versus Wrong, and Other Choices 77

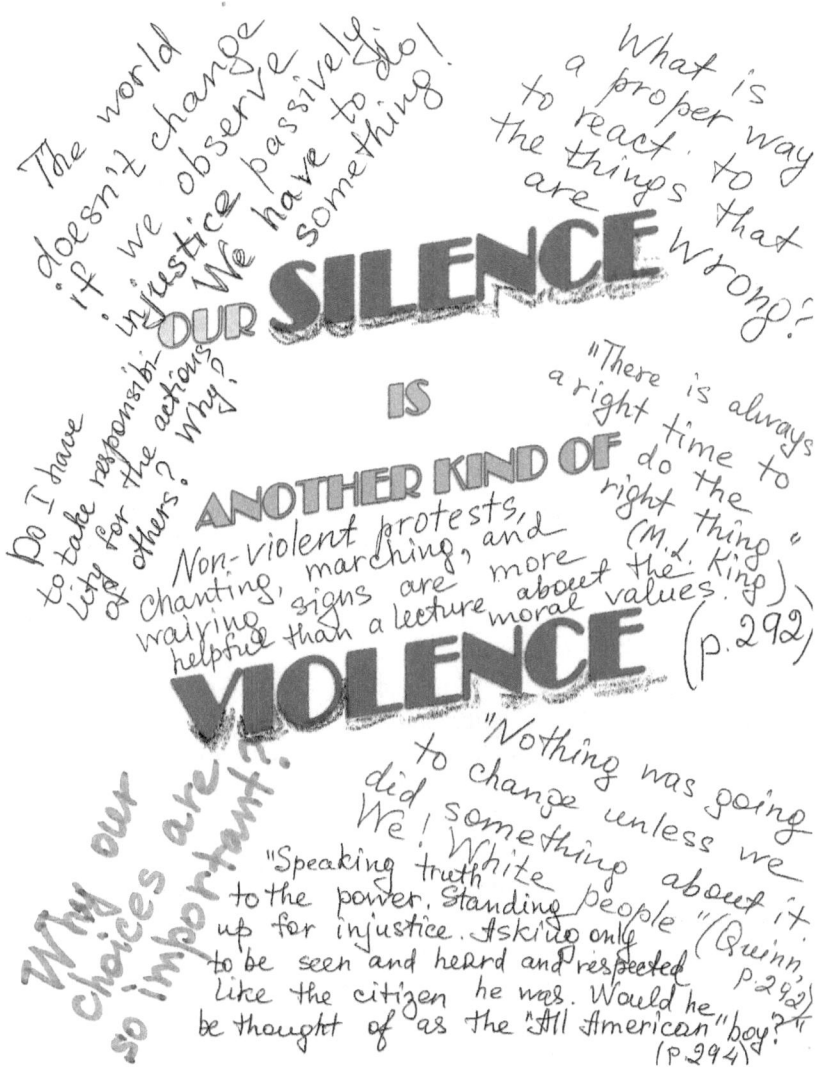

Figure 5.2 Graffity Activity Example. *Source:* Authors.

Chance Activity. Students complete this individual writing task after reading the novel and discussing the characters' choices and actions and their consequences. This task requires students to write about how it would change the story if a certain character had made a different decision earlier in the story. They may choose any character and any of the choices this character makes and rewrite the consequences of the decision. How would the story change? How would it affect other people and their decisions?

While students may choose one of the two protagonists' choices, it would be interesting to explore minor characters and their behavior. Students may choose characters and their decisions independently; however, if there are a couple of students who struggle to think of a situation, teachers may prepare two or three "what if" questions to help them start.

For example, what would happen if Carlos did not spray-paint the school's sidewalk with "Rashad Is Absent Again Today" graffiti? Other possibilities to examine are: What if Officer Paul Galuzzo publicly recognized his faulty assumptions and apologized for cruelly beating an innocent teenager? What if English Jones, Rashad's friend and Quinn's basketball teammate, did not question Quinn's position in the events? What if Jill, Paul and Guzzo's cousin, did not oppose her relatives and actively engage Quinn in the protest against police brutality?

Developing possible scenarios, similar to those suggested, allows students to think more about each important choice and see how it influences people around them, as well as how those choices may change the outcome of the situation. As an extension of this activity, teachers may organize a class discussion in which students analyze and evaluate their past choices and outcomes.

Argumentative Essay

A culminating assessment of the unit, along with the unit test, is an argumentative essay based on a literary analysis of the novel's major theme. By eleventh or twelfth grade, high schoolers know how to compose an argumentative piece of writing. They might need a brief refresher of the argument structure based on the specific expectations for the task at hand. Some teachers may include warrants and counterarguments or additional scholarly sources, and others may require developing an argument using solely the anchor novel.

It is necessary to remind readers that the best argumentative topics have a yes/no question at their core, thus making it possible to take a position (claim) and defend it (argue) using ample and reliable evidence. Favoring the 6+1 traits of writing, the argumentative prompt offered here follows the RAFTE strategy, meaning that students will get clear instructions on their **r**ole, **a**udience, **f**ormat of the paper, **t**opic, and **e**xpectations. It reads:

> Imagine that you are a literary critic writing an article to *Signal Journal* about the novel *All American Boys* (Reynolds & Kiely, 2015). In the form of an argument, explore the theme of choices and how it is developed in the novel. You may choose one or several characters to analyze their choices. Can these choices be categorized as good or bad and right or wrong? Present a clear, well-developed claim strongly outlining your position and sufficiently supporting it with textual evidence from the novel and other supplemental readings completed in class. Your

argumentative essay should be about 6–7 pages long and follow conventions of English language and MLA formatting style for citations and Works Cited page.

Working on this prompt, students follow all the steps of the writing process, improve their peer review skills, and enhance their argumentative writing. Most importantly, this chapter will serve as a final assessment of the teaching sequence and unit objectives and demonstrate students' understanding of the overarching concepts and essential questions.

Additional Learning Opportunities

The novel at the core of this unit offers a variety of additional learning prospects of engaging students in critical thinking, analysis, and interpretation. Teachers may develop mini-research projects asking students to investigate:

- censorship challenges that novels, similar to *All American Boys,* face in our society;
- various book awards and their criteria, including YALSA, Walden Award, Coretta Scott King Award, and other YA book awards; and
- other classic and young adult texts that develop the theme of Good versus Bad or Right versus Wrong.

There are several interviews with the authors, Reynolds and Kiely, and some of them are video recorded and available from YouTube. Teachers may include one or two partial interviews for students to watch in class and discuss the novel considering the authors' perspectives regarding the unit's theme. There is also potential for a creative writing project tasking students with "re-writing" one of the novel's minor characters, whether it is Rashad's father, Paul Galluzzo, Jill, one of Paul's cousins, or Quinn's mother. Explorations into the minor characters may help students realize their significance in developing main characters, themes, and plot.

UNIT MATERIALS INVENTORY

Anchor Text

Reynolds, J., and Kiely B. (2015). *All American Boys*. New York, NY: Simon & Schuster.

Short Stories:

Good Country People by Flannery O'Connor

After Twenty Years by O. Henry
Children of the Sea by Edwidge Danticat

Nonfiction

From *Resistance to Civil Government* by Henry David Thoreau
Change by Theodore Dreiser. Retrieved April 9, 2020, from https://americanliteratur e.com/author/theodore-dreiser/essay/change
The Sit-In Movement. Retrieved April 9, 2020, from https://www.commonlit.org/en/ texts/the-sit-in-movement

Poetry:

Dreams by Langston Hughes
The Road Not Taken by Robert Frost
There Is a Difference by William Henry Dawson
Choices by Nikki Giovanni
Hard Choices by Jojoba Mansell

YouTube Videos:

All American Boys co-authors Jason Reynolds and Brendan Kiely on race in America. Retrieved April 9, 2020, https://www.youtube.com/watch?v=RIJHGFbfiDw
MahoganyBooks Interviews Jason Reynolds & Brendan Kiely. Retrieved April 9, 2020, https://www.youtube.com/watch?v=_dnIejvYPJQ
Poems and Literature about Choice. Retrieved April 9, 2020, from http://www.grea texpectations.org/resources/poetry/poems-and-literature-about-choice/
Choices. An Interactive Short Film. Retrieved April 11, 2020, from https://www.you tube.com/watch?v=tPd8tD_G9ZU

ADDITIONAL RESOURCES FOR TEACHERS

The example of this teaching unit is based on *All American Boys* and supplemental readings and resources outlined in the previous sections. However, there are so many more texts and resources available to teachers today because the number of YA novels published every year is growing exponentially and because teachers and students have access to a multimodal variety of texts published online. Table 5.6 provides other possible fiction, nonfiction, and other media and web resources teachers may consider while developing their instructional sequence for thematic explorations of good, bad, right, wrong, and other choices.

Examination of Good versus Bad, Right versus Wrong, and Other Choices   81

Table 5.6   Additional Resources for Teachers

Fiction
Alexander, K. (2013). *He said, she said*. HarperCollins Publishers.
Forman, G. (2018). *I have lost my way*. Viking.
Ellis, D. (2012). *My Name Is Parvana*. Groundwood Books.
Yang, G.L. (2006). *American born Chinese*. First Second Books.
Nonfiction
Bicchieri, C. (2006). The grammar of society: The nature and dynamics of social norms. Cambridge University Press, Ch. 1.
Mackay, H. (2005). Right and wrong: How to decide for yourself. Hachette.
Albert, D., and Steinberg, L. (2011). Judgment and decision making in adolescence. *Journal of Research on Adolescence, 21*, 211–224
Media and Web Resources
Helping your child through early adolescence (2002). U.S. Department of Education. Retrieved April 17, 2020, https://www2.ed.gov/parents/academic/help/adolescence/adolescence.pdf
Enriquez, J. (2015). Is right and wrong always black and white? TEDxBeaconStreet. Retrieved April 17, 2020, https://www.youtube.com/watch?v=fcqhS1ExiBQ
McCue, J. (January, 2018). Why teenagers make terrible decisions: A guide for parents. ABC News. Retrieved April 17, 2020, https://www.abc.net.au/news/2018-01-22/why-teenagers-make-bad-decisions-a-parents-guide/9349084
Moral Practices—Ethical Standards—Right and Wrong Behavior (2020). Basic Knowledge 101. Retrieved April 17, 2020, https://www.basicknowledge101.com/categories/morality.html
Kohlberg, L. (1956). The Kohlberg dilemmas. CommonLit. Retrieved April 17, 2020, https://www.commonlit.org/en/texts/the-kohlberg-dilemmas

KEY ELEMENTS OF THE INSTRUCTIONAL UNIT

This chapter provides an example of a conceptual teaching unit based on thematic explorations of choices: good and bad, right and wrong, and other difficult decisions. The unit is designed using the common structure, including:

- a rationale and brief overview of the unit;
- unit concepts, essential questions, and objectives;
- a four-week calendar plan outlining major activities, strategies, and assignments;
- some examples of activities and projects that can be completed before, during, and after reading the anchor text;
- a list of literary texts used throughout the unit of study;
- additional or alternative resources to explore the theme.

This unit example might be used in its entirety or modified and adjusted depending on the school's culture, student population, and available resources.

Chapter 6

Self-Perception and Being Oneself

THEMATIC CONTEXT AND TRADITIONAL APPROACHES

One of the most imperative parts of adolescence is the construction of self-perception. Adolescence is a key time period for this development of self-perception, which can include self-image, body image, confidence, fitting in versus standing out, and so forth. Self-perception, in its turn, is complicated by a variety of factors, including language, gender and sexuality, representations in media and popular culture, and other social constructs.

As a result, adolescents' paths to developing a positive self-perception can be complicated, can include a number of ebbs and flows, and can be influenced by both internal and external factors. Thus, including self-perception as a literary theme of study in secondary ELA classrooms presents authentic and relevant opportunities to not only engage in rigorous literary analysis but also grow as individuals.

This theme and chapter intersect with chapter 2 on identity search and can help students develop and layer their senses of self across a course of study. To continue students' quest for self-discovery, the discussion of self-perception here focuses more specifically on courage and facing reality, on finding strength to be self-confident, on self-reliance, self-acceptance, and self-worth. The study of self-perception often includes ideas of finding and creating places to belong, developing and drawing on one's inner strength, and embracing and facing changes with courage and confidence.

The discussion of self-perception in this chapter also connects with chapter 4 on examining the universal theme of Good versus Bad, Right versus Wrong, and other difficult choices young adults make on a daily basis. The choices young people make reflect their understanding of these universal concepts, which are a crucial part of developing self-perception, including courage, self-acceptance, and self-worth. The ways all the three themes—self-discovery, making choices, and self-perception—interrelate and build on one another create more powerful, nuanced, and multilayered opportunities for students to meaningfully analyze literature and to apply that analysis and reflection to their own lives.

Developing Self-Perception

Adolescents develop their self-perception first and foremost in relation to others around them. During this stage of their lives, young people begin to compare themselves to others, and they begin to recognize that other adolescents do the same to them. They consider positive and negative responses and perceptions from those around them, and they compare that against how they currently view themselves, using that information to make conscious (and subconscious) decisions to tweak, alter, and revise how they present to the world, with the ultimate, and sometimes competing, goals of being accepted by others and accepting themselves.

These external perceptions and the ways adolescents respond to them become even more complex when considering that often, youth believe that the perceptions others hold of them do not match what they know about themselves (e.g., gender identity, ethnicity). Such dissonance complicates the processes of developing a positive self-perception and self-construction as a reaction to the way young people perceive themselves. In short, external factors play major roles, both helpful and competing, in how adolescents see themselves and how they interact with the world.

The process of developing self-perception inevitably includes using external factors as criteria for one's personal growth; that is, adolescents consider themselves through an external lens first as they become self-aware by collecting information from the sources around them, and that self-awareness or self-concept/perception continues to develop through collecting more and more information from more and more experiences and interactions with others. As a result, adolescents, as well as humans in general, gain a sense of belonging based on how adults and other peers view and treat them.

After considering the external response, they are able to use an internal self-evaluation mechanism. If the world around them is more acceptable and appreciative, it may lead youth to believe in themselves, to feel more stable and secure, to relieve pressure—whether self-imposed or otherwise—and to perceive their existence as more manageable and more comfortable. In the opposite case, the situation may intensify negative self-perception and bring more insecurities, low self-esteem, lack of confidence, desire to alienate, and/or attempt to change in order to be accepted.

Self-Perception as Relevant Literary Theme

The study of self-perception as a literary theme, one leading to greater understanding of and comfort with one's self, can include a variety of components. Engaging in this unit of study can allow students to examine societal instances of tolerance and intolerance, of affirmation and devaluing, of those who are different. Relatedly, focusing on self-perception requires readers to turn that reflective light inward and consider what roles their own tolerance/intolerance play in their own development. At the heart of this self-exploration is the intersection of self-concept and group identity via labels, social "norms," popular beliefs, expectations, and so forth. This serves as a reminder of the importance of creating instructional space for students to use texts toward their own self-growth and development.

While this theme may be taught using a multitude of texts, one often-taught canonical text, with the theme of self-perception at its center, is *To Kill a Mockingbird* (Lee, 1960, 2014). This is certainly not the only classic text used to teach this theme—see also *Great Expectations* (Dickens, Law, & Pinnington, 1998), *The Great Gatsby* (Fitzgerald, 1925, 2004), *Pride and Prejudice* (Austen, 1995), and so forth—but it serves as the focal text for the discussion in this chapter. Lee's novel has been a curricular fixture for generations in ELA classrooms, and many current teachers grew up reading and loving the novel themselves.

Recently, Lee's novel has been criticized by many scholars and pedagogues for the ways race, racism, and privilege are portrayed, all reasons to interrogate this and other texts traditionally taught in ELA classrooms. But problematic perpetuation of the White savior narrative and outdated messages aside, *To Kill a Mockingbird* also falls short of helping all, or even most, students consider and engage in their own development of self-perception, suggesting teachers continue to consider other powerful texts for use in their classrooms.

Much of the novel is about Scout's (the story's narrator) own self-perception and the ways she better understands herself in relation to those people and experiences around her. That is, Scout provides readers a view of one young girl, how she perceives herself, and how that self-perception, whether realistic or not, influences her views of (and on) the world. In the beginning of the novel, Scout begins as innocent and ignorant, largely, to society and the realities it includes. In large part, she is a relatively flat character, one who remains fairly constant throughout the narrative.

In fact, her agency as a character and as an individual is almost entirely absent. Her father is mostly credited for who she is, taking any agency, development, and true self-perception away from her. Rather than a character who evolves, learns more about herself, and gains confidence, Scout is positioned as the embodiment of innocence, making it difficult for students to recognize themselves in her experiences, actions, and development. While a number of critical lenses, such as Critical Race Theory, First and Second Wave Whiteness Studies, and so on, can be applied to Scout and to this novel, leading to deep and important literary study, self-perception as a relevant lens for students falls short of applicability.

Throughout the novel, Scout, in essence, moves from a child's view of the world to that of an adult. Rather than considering the world through the eyes and experiences of a grade-school student, which makes it all the more complicated for readers to believe how she is able to see and analyze the world around her, she is positioned as wise, wiser than the adults. This can lead to Scout, as a character, coming across as unnatural or even superficial, preventing readers from viewing her as a model of self-perception development and limiting the ways they can personally connect to the text and grow as a result. In this way, readers get a better sense of how she views the outside world than of how she views herself, which, again, serves as a barrier to students' using Scout's experiences to drive their own evolutions.

She grows to understand more of those around her than she does of herself and her own growth and development. In many ways, it can be argued, Scout functions less as a dynamic character and more as a literary device, allowing readers to observe the world through her eyes and innocence, making it considerably more difficult for them to consider the ways their selves—their experiences and beliefs, the ways others view and have impacted them—influence how they view the world.

Finally, *To Kill a Mockingbird* does not take into account nonlinear paths to self-perception. In other words, Scout's path to realization and to self-development follows a largely uninterrupted and singular pattern and does not acknowledge the myriad and plural ways adolescents interact with the world and use those experiences to better understand themselves. Even though she experiences the horrors of racism in the South, she has little ebb and flow to her growth, a process that does not align well with how actual young people develop in iterative and *complex ways, or as they experience the world.*

DRAWING CONNECTIONS TO STUDENTS' LIVES

Many traditional ways of attempting to engage students in meaningful and personally relevant literary study of the development of self-perception may fall short of truly reaching each student and offering them characters and situations in which they can relate and draw meaning. This chapter, for example, provides a look at one often-taught canonical text, Lee's *To Kill a Mockingbird*, and the ways it offers a limited view of and an opportunity to study self-perception which might be challenging to connect to contemporary students' lives, experiences, and contexts.

Like any other literary theme (e.g., those discussed in chapters 2 and 4 in this text), it is vital for students to have access to characters, stories, and experiences with which they can see themselves or see parallels to themselves and the lives they lead. As a result, teachers are tasked with getting to really know their students and using that knowledge to select relevant and powerful literary texts and to design purposeful instruction meant to bring those texts and their students together for the purposes of deep literary analysis and personal self-reflection.

Similar to the discussion in Chapter 2, teachers can begin this process by reflecting on a few helpful questions. Why and in what ways do I want students to develop their self-perception? How can I use text selection and instructional design to foster an environment where students engage in this personal and vulnerable developmental work? How might I create a space that respects and welcomes plural views of the self, and what would such a space look like and include? In what ways can I position the literary study of self-perception to simultaneously foster growth as human beings and development of transferable English language arts skills?

Once those questions have been answered, the next step is to consider pedagogical and methodological tools to create successful learning experiences. The ultimate goal is to design instruction, including text selection, that both connects to students' lives and lived experiences and fosters deep academic study of the literary theme. Given the myriad of differences in students and contexts, a great variety of diverse young adult novels written in different perspectives and formats, this chapter offers teachers a look at Gene Yang's *American Born Chinese* (2006) as one potential text useful for achieving these goals. What follows is a discussion and rationale for making relevance and student connections to texts central to the study of self-perception.

Before moving on, it should also be noted that Yang's graphic novel is but one of the many powerful and complex texts available to teachers, including many with characters who identify as girls or young women, who identify as LGBTQ, and/or who are marginalized because of their racial, ethnic, or socioeconomic background. A comprehensive list of these texts is impossible here, but the following YAL novels can easily be dropped into this discussion and subsequent example unit in place of *American Born Chinese*:

- *Smile* (2010) by Raina Telgemeier
- *Catalyst* (2003) by Laurie Halse Anderson
- *Someday This Pain Will Be Useful to You* (2007) by Peter Cameron
- *Dear Martin* (2017) by Nic Stone
- *Darius the Great Is Not Okay* (2018) by Adib Khorram

Through a literary investigation of Yang's graphic novel, an investigation centered around self-perception, students will, through analyzing characters, come to draw on their own inner strength, face difficulties with courage, and ultimately create their own sense of belonging. Spending time focused on this thematic unit can create space for adolescents to recognize the inherent difficulty in finding inner strength and that building and sustaining inner strength is a lifetime process. By connecting with characters who draw on inner strength to assist them in navigating difficult decisions and experiences, young people will be better positioned to find ways to do this themselves—that is, to make conscious decisions to utilize the strengths that lie within them.

Part of drawing on one's inner strength involves facing difficulties with courage. Literary study provides a robust space for students to analyze the courage various characters apply to situations in their lives. These analytical experiences can be transferred to students' lives via reflective interrogation. Interacting with quality literature helps students to understand that everyone has inner strength and courage, even if it looks and manifests differently, and that those around them can contribute to developing self-perception and confidence and applying courage to the situations they encounter.

Lastly, a thematic focus on self-perception opens space to question the ways challenges shape individuals, both positively and negatively, and how one's response is connected to their own senses of self. While engaged in this type of thematic unit, students consider where and how they belong. This includes how they view others, how they view themselves through others' eyes, and how others view them. Recognizing that everyone experiences challenges and doubt and that those seemingly negative experiences are part of adolescent development is crucial. Ultimately, studying self-perception offers students a path to self-acceptance accompanied by self-construction and to carving out their own spaces in the world.

The following two sections present a brief overview of *American Born Chinese* (Yang, 2006), the graphic novel serving as the anchor text for this unit and thematic analysis, and a discussion of how it can be used to engage students in rigorous literary study of the development of self-perception and in their own critical reflection on and growth toward how they view and perceive themselves. Chapter 7, then, provides one example instructional unit designed to help students make personal connections and grow as individuals through the study of one literary theme.

GRAPHIC NOVEL OVERVIEW: *AMERICAN BORN CHINESE* BY GENE LUEN YANG (2006)

American Born Chinese is an award-winning (e.g., 2006 National Book Award Honor Book, 2007 Michael L. Printz Award) graphic novel that weaves together three seemingly separate narratives. The first presents a version of the ancient Chinese myth of the Monkey King. The second narrative is the story of Jin Wang, a student in San Francisco, who wrestles with his own identity as a Chinese American.

The third narrative is about Danny, a teen, who is drawn as White, with an embarrassing cousin named Chin-Kee. Each of the three narratives traces individual plot lines, characters, and experiences, but in the end of the text, Yang brings these together into one larger story of identity and self-perception.

Throughout the text, each character's self-perception is driven, in part, by those around them. That is, the ways they are viewed and treated by others serve as powerful variables influencing how they feel about and view themselves. The Monkey King is influenced by the other deities in his circle. Jin is impacted by the White students at his new school. And Danny appears constantly embarrassed by how he believes others will view his cousin, and by connection himself.

In this way, *American Born Chinese* is similar to de la Peña's *Mexican Whiteboy* (discussed in chapter 2) in that characters in both novels feel excluded from certain identity groups, depending on the perceptions and actions of others. This sense of exclusion impacts how they see and understand themselves. Both novels offer students opportunities to analyze the experiences of marginalized people of color and the influence of whiteness, privilege, and systemic racism on young people, culture, and education. Likewise, novels and characters such as these create space for teachers to engage in antiracist teaching, learning, and acting in their classrooms (see, e.g., Borsheim-Black & Sarigianides, 2019).

YAL AND THEMATIC EXPLORATION: *AMERICAN BORN CHINESE* AND BEING OURSELVES

While engaging with the graphic novel, readers follow three overlapping narratives and characters who, throughout their experiences, come to better understand themselves, especially in relation to those around them. Each of the three characters, in their own ways, begins to develop a more positive self-perception and self-worth, often pushing through their own struggles to appreciate and value themselves. In the end, once they are able to see clearly who they each are individually and how they have each influenced the others, all three characters are more clearly able to see themselves for who they really are.

As a result, students can analyze the actions, decisions, and development of the Monkey King, Jin, and Danny as they progress through their individual stories and across the intersections of each. Students, for example, can see that the Monkey King battles jealousy, which leads to anger and questionable decisions. In an effort to be an acknowledged and respected member alongside the other gods, he attempts to make himself simultaneously equal to and greater than all others.

Students can, as part of their analysis, trace major changes in the Monkey King. Early in the story, he is full of pride and is driven by his ego. Readers may note that this ego, or attempts to reposition himself, is a byproduct of how he considers himself in relation to those around him. In persuading others of his dominance, the Monkey King mistakenly believes that he can convince himself, as individuals do not exist in isolation, that challenges are only overcome through relationships with the other. It forces him to lose sight of who he really is, and it ends up literally holding him prisoner until he is finally able to truly believe in himself and take his true form.

In the second narrative, students can follow Jin's development and consider it against their own. In his narrative, Jin begins to view himself in response to many of his interactions with those outside his family—at school, with friends, with teachers, and so on. In other words, the ways outsiders perceive him play important roles in how he perceives himself. Throughout the story, this is often manifested as White people's assumptions, stereotypes, and ignorance about Chinese culture and, for that matter, any culture different from their own White, Christian-normative ways of living and believing.

As is noted in the title of the graphic novel, Jin struggles to reconcile his Chinese heritage with his American-ness. That is, he feels pulled in different directions and often doesn't feel as if he fits in with either. Jin's desire to transform and become someone other than himself and his future metamorphosis toward acceptance respecting his identity is clearly demonstrated by his obsession with a Transformer toy, a toy that can take on multiple shapes and become multiple things depending on what a situation calls for. The Chinese herbalist responds to Jin's revelation by saying, "It's easy to become anything you wish . . . so long as you're willing to forfeit your soul" (Yang, p. 29). Reading this, students can analyze the symbol of the Transformer, interrogate Jin's internal struggle and the impact it has on his feelings of self-worth and self-concept, and make connections to their own experiences becoming different people.

Jin sees himself as different from the White students, from the Asian students in his classes, and from all those around him. He sees himself as entirely different, as not really fitting into his school, community, or cultural environments. Similarly, Jin defines himself based on how he views others such as those teachers and students around him. This complicated desire to belong and be accepted parallels adolescents' development, and as such, students can use Jin's narrative to reflect meaningfully on their own senses of acceptance. Eventually, such a reflection allows readers to begin questioning their own constructions and conceptions of self and their own struggles to develop positive self-perception.

Similarly to the Monkey King and Jin, Danny also grapples with who he is, how he is viewed by others, and how, in relation, he views himself. This presents a uniquely powerful opportunity for students reading *American Born Chinese*. Rather than analyzing the experiences of one character and working to make personal connections to those experiences, as is true with many traditional narratives and which can certainly be beneficial, Yang's graphic novel offers three unique benefits.

First, students are introduced to three main characters, each with their own stories, their own contexts and situations, and their own development of self-perception. Second, the graphic novel format provides visual context and the power of images for students to make connections to and to build understandings of, reflections on, and relationships to and between the Monkey King, Jin, and Danny. Third, and perhaps most importantly, readers are able to relate to both Jin's and Danny's struggles with identity and self-acceptance, and they are later able to make connections to them as competing sides of the same person. Both of these characters, similar to many adolescents regardless of situation, are desperate to fit into social and institutional norms and to see themselves as part of something larger.

Comparably to many teens, Danny wrestles with the embarrassment he feels over his cousin, Chin-Kee. Chin-Kee represents a side of Danny he would rather his peers not see, one he clearly harbors embarrassment over, and as a result, his cousin impacts his self-perception, that is, the way he sees himself in relation to external norms or expectations. Analyzing Danny, students can consider the worry he feels about how his friends and teammates may perceive him and whether or not he will be/feel welcomed in those peer groups. Similarly, students can consider the ways Danny's concerns over how he is perceived impacts how he acts and progresses throughout the story.

This analysis can allow students to better understand Danny as a character and his development of self-perception and concept, but it can also aid them in reflecting on their own lives and their own embarrassment and concern over parts of themselves they are not yet comfortable with. Danny's concerns, much like those of adolescent readers, play weighty roles in how he feels about himself and how he perceives himself. Through analyzing Danny's experiences, students can come to better understand themselves and to view themselves through an asset-based lens, rather than one highlighting deficits.

Here, students can make connections back to chapter 2 and the journey of self-discovery. Similar to the traditional hero's quest, Danny experiences, challenges, and, in many ways, his own downfall were followed by a victory over his own insecurities. As part of this analysis and connection to a previous theme, students can recognize how Danny's journey leads him to self-discovery, to self-perception, and to self-acceptance as he finally embraces who he is and finally recognizes that he is going to be okay.

Yang's graphic novel, as is outlined here, serves as a relevant and complex text for use in any ELA classroom, specifically with regard to thematic study of the development of self-perception. The three overlapping narratives offer students multiple points of connection, a variety of experiences with and approaches to character growth and self-perception, and powerful visuals that provide context and offer yet another way for students to relate to the text. In these ways, *American Born Chinese* offers readers a layered and even cross-thematic analytical opportunities, one sign of a truly complex and powerful text.

KEY IDEAS

This chapter introduces the literary theme of self-perception. Readers are introduced to the concept of self-perception, the ways it is connected to adolescent development, and a rationale for its inclusion in literary study.

Analogous to chapters 2 and 4, the chapter discusses a traditional text, Harper Lee's *To Kill a Mockingbird*, and the ways it falls short of (1) connecting to all students and (2) effectively representing the complexity of self-perception development.

Finally, it offers a rationale for bringing in the contemporary graphic novel *American Born Chinese* (Yang, 2006) to more meaningfully engage students in literary analysis of self-perception and in their own individual development toward positive self-perception.

The subsequent chapter offers readers an example instructional unit using Yang's graphic novel as the anchor text. The sample unit is designed to engage students in literary study of and personal reflection into the development of self-perception, including all the internal and external variables contributing to such development.

Chapter 7

Conceptual Teaching Unit
Developing a Positive Self-Perception

The example literary unit described in this chapter can work with students in grades 8–12, but it is framed specifically here for a ninth-grade ELA class. Ninth grade students are in a unique phase of change in their lives, as they transition from young adolescence and middle school to their teenage years and the final four years of their public schooling. During this time, teens are often still learning about themselves, considering themselves in relation to those around them, and developing shifting perceptions of self. Engaging ninth graders in a literary study around self-perception offers a potentially powerful space for self-analysis and personal growth.

While the example unit below is designed with ninth grade students in mind, it can be easily tweaked to accommodate middle school classrooms as well, especially at the eighth grade level. The transition from young adolescence to adolescence encompasses physical, cognitive, and social-emotional growth, and it is just as important to provide younger students opportunities to consider how their self-perception develops and what factors influence it. The bulk of this unit can be adapted with minimal change and implemented in grades 6–8 classrooms, but teachers may choose to alter how the reading is chunked, the scaffolding provided, and the amount of time spent building background knowledge as they engage younger students in similar literary study.

As noted in previous chapters, it is important that teachers consider ways to use the study of literature (e.g., a unit built around studying self-perception in YAL) as a vehicle for self-reflection and for students to analyze themselves and their own lives. To that end, the example literary unit in this chapter is intended to foster literary character analysis on the road to analysis of self.

As emphasized throughout this book, teachers are the experts of their own contexts. Thus, they know best how to engage and encourage their students in generative ways. They know best how to sequence and scaffold instruction for their students, in their classrooms. Instructional decisions, in other words, should rest in the hands of classroom teachers. The example unit described below is just that—an example, one meant to provide teachers with ideas, potential directions, and ultimately a starting point for their own instructional design purposes.

This unit on self-perception would work well toward the end of a course for a variety of reasons. Adolescents' development of self-perception takes time. Youth often continue in this development throughout young adolescence and across the teen years. As a result, this unit can be a sort of culminating experience after a semester or year of analyzing literature. Connecting back to chapter 3, where the unit on identity was positioned early in the semester/year, the unit described here could be part of the same course and used to, in some ways, book-end students' learning experiences.

After forming clearer identities, students could then apply those as powerful lenses to all other texts they read and analyze throughout the year, leading up to perhaps a final unit on self-perception, where students take all their experiences across the course and combine them with their deep study of *American Born Chinese* to finish the year with a stronger and more positive sense of who they are as people and of the value they bring to the world.

Building on the discussion of self-perception as a component of adolescent development in chapter 6, this chapter offers an example unit of literary study designed to guide students along their paths to positive self-perception. The anchor text selected for this unit is Gene Yang's (2006) *American Born Chinese*, an award-winning and brilliant graphic novel that weaves together three overlapping and related narratives. Reading about, discussing, and analyzing the decisions, actions, and development of the Monkey King, Jin, and Danny, students recognize the multifaceted nature of self-perception and the countless factors, both internal and external, impacting it.

Connected to Yang's graphic novel and to layer students' experiences, the unit also includes a range of other texts and text types. For example, in order to further provide students with representations of self-perception development, factors impacting how humans see themselves, settings, and scenarios that play a role in the ways young people wrestle with who they are, students will engage with other graphic novels (in whole and excerpted form), poetry and music, excerpts from short stories and novels, informational texts, and so forth.

This example unit also includes a second anchor text—Marjane Satrapi's graphic memoir *Persepolis*. In the narrative, Satrapi describes her and her family's experiences in Iran in the early 1980s. Throughout the text, she shares why and how the government, education as an institution, family, and so forth influence who she is, who she becomes, and both how she perceives herself and the ways she responds.

Satrapi's graphic narrative connects well to Yang's text and to the theme of self-perception. By reading (and viewing) both texts, students are able to consider the multiple ways individuals are impacted by the contexts in which they find themselves. The different storylines complicate any misconceptions students might have of a linear or singular path to positively perceiving oneself. Together, the two graphic novels also serve as different mentor texts for students as they craft their own graphic narratives.

Similar to the discussion of text selection and decisions around when teachers could implement this or a similar unit, the activities and assignments selected for inclusion in this example unit were chosen intentionally to (1) connect to the readings and (2) help guide students through their learning and development with regard to self-perception.

In conjunction with reading and discussion experiences, students are provided with a range of opportunities to use composing as a tool for reflection, connection, meaning-making, and personal growth and development. These composing experiences range from regular journal entries to a graphic narrative to a letter to self, all selected to guide students through pre-reading, during-reading, and after-reading critical thought and analysis.

With regard to assessment, the unit includes a range of methods for teacher and self-assessment. Journal entries, for example, can serve as useful formative assessment, throughout the entirety of the unit, for both the teacher and the student. Activities and assignments such as the letter to self, while certainly helpful for teachers, are inherently reflective and self-focused in nature, providing students powerful moments of self-analysis.

Finally, the culminating project, the graphic narrative, while requiring students to reflect on themselves and their growth, can act as an assessment allowing teachers to see evidence of textual analysis as a representation of connecting texts to their own lives and as a lens for viewing student growth.

OVERARCHING CONCEPTS, ESSENTIAL QUESTIONS, AND UNIT OBJECTIVES

Building off the thematic discussion in chapter 6, the sample teaching unit described in this chapter is designed around self-perception and helping students to use literary analysis as a tool for coming to better view, understand, and appreciate themselves. Specifically, this unit utilizes Gene Yang's *American Born Chinese* as the anchor text. Combined with other pieces of literature, nonfiction texts, discussions, and opportunities for composition, students can analyze the self-perception development of the Monkey King, Jin, and Danny and begin applying those to their own lives.

The unit discussed below draws on the concepts of adolescent development of self-concept and self-perception and the ways these are impacted by how youth view others and are viewed by those around them. This concept is described in more detail in chapter 6. Engaging with literature, such as

Yang's award-winning graphic novel, around these developmental concepts creates time, space, and support for students to (1) further develop their literary analysis skills and (2) take an active role in their own growth with regard to self-perception.

Entering this unit, students will have read a variety of literature in earlier grades that deal with self-perception as a theme (e.g., *Brown Girl Dreaming* (2014) by Jacqueline Woodson, *Nimona* (2015) by Noelle Stevenson, *El Deafo* (2014) by Cece Bell, *Ghost* (2017) by Jason Reynolds, *The Skin I'm In* (1999) by Sharon G. Flake, *Inside Out and Back Again* (2011) by Thanhha Lai). Many middle grades books, for example, include this theme, so students at the high school level most likely have experience reading and discussing related texts. Similarly, because one key component to adolescent development involves recognizing relationships between self and others, students will benefit from a unit focused specifically on self-perception.

Using young adult literature as a lens, students can begin to recognize relationships between the characters and settings they read about and their own lives and contexts. Experiences analyzing and discussing how characters navigate the development of self-perception are transferable skills, helping secondary students to shine that analytical light on themselves and better understand where they have been, where they are, and where they are going. Students, for example, can recognize the ways literary characters position themselves for growth and consider how they, as individuals, might borrow from those characters and take active roles in their own development.

Through engaging in this literary study, students can ultimately better understand themselves and the factors impacting how they view themselves. Adolescents' self-perceptions are influenced not only by the ways they view the world and others in their lives but also by the ways they are viewed by others. This unit is designed to help students question these developmental variables and understand the factors influential in their self-perception and then ultimately to use thoughtful and intentional reflection to better understand and more clearly "see" themselves. The following essential questions will frame this unit and serve as catalysts to student learning and growth:

- What active role(s) do I play in developing a self-perception?
- In what ways does self-perception change? What factors contribute to its ebbs and flows?
- How is my self-perception and sense of self-worth influenced by others?
- How does better understanding influential factors for self-perception help me to better understand and view myself?
- In what ways does my self-perception impact my decisions and actions?

Developing a Positive Self-Perception

In addition to grappling with the essential questions and engaging in meaningful literary analysis, students will use writing, including multimodal composition, to reflect, to learn, to grow, and to demonstrate their progression on unit standards and objectives. Throughout the unit, students will be able to:

- read and understand complex texts;
- cite relevant textual evidence that supports analysis;
- identify one or more themes in literary works;
- analyze theme development through point of view, settings, and plot;
- analyze how complex characters develop over the course of a text;
- compose well-developed constructed responses to the texts;
- develop a multimodal personal narrative using images, alphabetic text, and comic/graphic novel techniques;
- demonstrate the use of the writing process to strengthen writing;
- write for different lengths of time for a range of tasks;
- participate in a variety of whole-class and small-group discussions about the text; and
- understand academic vocabulary.

The following section presents a sample calendar plan for a four-week unit on self-perception. The goal of this sample plan is to help teachers map out instructional strategies, activities, and assessments in one example of a logical progression.

CALENDAR PLAN FOR A CONCEPTUAL TEACHING UNIT

To assist teachers with considering a full literary unit on self-perception and to serve as a frame for daily lesson planning, this section provides a unit at a glance, or a unit overview calendar plan, laying out breakdowns of readings, sequencing of sample unit activities and assignments, and offering a starting point for classroom teachers interested in teaching a similar unit. This calendar plan is also intended to share a range of possible instructional activities and strategies and to demonstrate one way these can be sequenced to foster student learning and development.

The calendar plan presented here includes pre- and self-assessment early on, allowing students to consider what they already know about the theme and to begin questioning their current self-perceptions. Journaling—character and image analyses—are woven throughout the unit and serve as a daily touchpoint for students. The journal entries will also be available to students as they begin to work on the two main culminating projects, the letter to self and the graphic narrative. The goal is to help students build their understandings and skills daily and to use those to better understand themselves.

While *American Born Chinese* is the anchor text, students will also read a significant portion of Marjane Satrapi's graphic novel *Persepolis*. Readings from both texts are assigned together, offering students layered looks at character development and a variety of ways others, situations, experiences, and selves can influence how one perceives themselves. In addition to serving as literary texts, both graphic novels also become mentor texts for students who are, as a conclusion to the unit, tasked with crafting their own graphic narratives representing their own development of self-perception across the unit (Tables 7.1–7.5).

The goal of Week 1 is to introduce students to the unit theme and the variety of assignments they will be completing over the coming weeks. Similarly, Week 1 introduces students to the anchor text, *American Born Chinese*, and a second graphic novel, *Persepolis*, from which they will be reading excerpts. In short, this is a foundational week designed to get students thinking about self-perception and to provide them a basis on which to build their learning and development over the coming four weeks.

Table 7.1   Week 1

Monday	Unit Introduction Journal Entry: How do you view yourself, and what do you believe contributes to how you see yourself?
	Introduce Unit
	Class Discussion: What is self-perception?
	Read, analyze, and discuss poem: "Identity" by Julio Noboa Polanco
Tuesday	Unit Introduction Journal Entry: How do you believe others view you, and how do others' perceptions influence how you view yourself?
	Pre-reading Activity: Complete Self-Portrait
	View video: "The Power of Self-Perception"
Wednesday	Pre-reading Activity: Write Personal Mission Statement
	Introduce Anchor Text: *American Born Chinese*
	Introduce Supplemental Text: *Persepolis*
Thursday	Introduce Character Analysis Journal
	Introduce Image Analysis Journal
	For Homework: Read *American Born Chinese* (pp. 1–20) and *Persepolis* (pp. 3–9)
Friday	Model and practice character analysis and image analysis journals: gradual release model
	View video: "The Psychology of Your Future Self"
	For Homework: Read *American Born Chinese* (pp. 22–40) and *Persepolis* (pp. 26–32)

Table 7.2   Week 2

Monday	Character Analysis Journal Entry Image Analysis Journal Entry Class Discussion and Activity Topics: • What initial connections to self-perception are you beginning to see in and across the two texts? • At this point, how can you relate to the characters in *American Born Chinese* and *Persepolis*? • What predictions can you make? For Homework: Read *American Born Chinese* (pp. 43–52) and *Persepolis* (pp. 111–117)
Tuesday	Character Analysis Journal Entry Image Analysis Journal Entry Class Discussion and Activity Topics: • Analyze Danny and Chin-Kee's first meeting • Why is Danny so embarrassed by his cousin, especially in front of a girl he appears to like? • What does this embarrassment tell us about Danny's self-perception, about how he views himself in that moment? • In small groups, note any similarities and differences you see between Danny and Marjane For Homework: Complete a Venn Diagram based on the small group discussions in class.
Wednesday	Character Analysis Journal Entry Image Analysis Journal Entry Class Discussion and Activity Topics: • How would mastering the Four Disciplines (those the Monkey King masters) influence your life? In what ways might it alter who you are and how you view yourself? • Group analysis of the Monkey King's hubris: how does he contribute to his imprisonment? • Have you ever been guilty of causing your own trouble? • In small groups, create a Venn Diagram of the Monkey King's and Marjane's choices and the impact of those choices For Homework: Read *American Born Chinese* (pp. 53–84) and *Persepolis* (pp. 126–134)
Thursday	Character Analysis Journal Entry Image Analysis Journal Entry Class Discussion and Activity Topics: • Discuss Jin's "first love." In what ways does caring for/about another influence self-perception? • Reflect on a time you've been jealous of someone else. What were you jealous of? Why do you think you were jealous? What came of that feeling (i.e., how did it impact you and those you felt jealousy toward)? • In what ways do Jin and Marjane alter their appearances, and what factors contribute to those changes? • Class list of reasons teens choose to alter their appearance For Homework: Read *American Born Chinese* (pp. 85–106) and *Persepolis* (pp. 164–172)

(Continued)

Table 7.2 Week 2 (*Continued*)

Friday	Character Analysis Journal Entry Image Analysis Journal Entry Class Discussion and Activity Topics: • Group analysis: the role(s) of context on self-perception • What makes Danny so concerned about his school peers meeting/seeing Chin-Kee? In other words, why is he so afraid of his two worlds colliding? • Create a graphic organizer of the reasons Danny is worried about how others perceive him and the consequences he believes could follow • In small groups: How are stereotypes enacted in and around Danny's and Marjane's lives? How have you seen stereotypes enacted here at school? For Homework: Read *American Born Chinese* (pp. 107–130) and *Persepolis* (pp. 189–197)

While building on the groundwork of Week 1, the instruction and experiences in Week 2 are also somewhat foundational, at least in the sense that students will just be getting into the readings and will just be beginning to consider the literary characters as individuals. Through Week 2 readings, discussions, and activities, students will gain experience using a close reading of texts and of applying textual concepts to themselves, a skill they will build on throughout the remainder of the unit.

Week 3 provides students opportunities to build on the previous two weeks and to dive more deeply into their analyses of literary characters. Moreover, Week 3 will serve as a more explicit and intentional springboard toward using their readings and experiences in the unit to reflect on themselves as humans. Students' textual and self-analyses in Week 3 will strengthen their skills and foundation as they enter Weeks 4 and 5, where they are tasked with articulating all they have learned and the ways they have grown through composing about themselves.

Week 4 picks up where Week 3 left off. As students finish their unit readings and begin working on their culminating assignments, they will continue to shine the reflective light inward and to consider how these texts, the characters, and the instructional experiences they have had are impacting how they view themselves—that is, how they are developing toward positive self-perception. In Week 5, students will continue using reflection and textual evidence to further craft and draft their culminating compositions.

In Week 5, students will continue to take all they have learned throughout the unit and apply it to themselves. This week is all about composing to and for the self. As students work on their graphic narratives and compose their Letters to Self, they will articulate exactly who they are at this moment, how they have grown and developed over the previous few weeks, and how they perceive themselves as a result.

Table 7.3 Week 3

Monday	Character Analysis Journal Entry
	Image Analysis Journal Entry
	Class Discussion and Activity Topics:
	• Analyzing the Monkey King: What evidence do we see that he becomes enlightened and finally recognizes his relation to others? How does he ultimately free himself of his self-imposed (or at least self-maintained) prison?
	• What personal connections have you made to the Monkey King's path to self-perception? How might Marjane see connections to her life?
	For Homework: Read *American Born Chinese* (pp. 131–160) and *Persepolis* (pp. 223–232)
Tuesday	Character Analysis Journal Entry
	Image Analysis Journal Entry
	Class Discussion and Activity Topics:
	• Group Discussion: We've seen a good bit of embarrassment from characters thus far, so in what ways does Jin's embarrassment and second guessing of himself impact his experiences and how he sees himself?
	• Reflect on the passive-aggressive racism Jin experiences. Why is he asked to leave Amelia alone so that she isn't negatively influenced by him? What does this experience do to his evolving self-perception? Make sure to note any times you have seen or experienced something similar
	• Create a timeline of events that contribute to Jin becoming/seeing himself as Danny
	For Homework: Read *American Born Chinese* (pp. 161–198) and *Persepolis* (pp. 246–257)
Wednesday	Character Analysis Journal Entry
	Image Analysis Journal Entry
	Class Discussion and Activity Topics:
	• Sketch out two versions of your own identity. If these two were to battle, how might that battle end?
	• How does battling with one's self, one's multiple perceived identities, contribute to (positively or negatively) the development of self-perception?
	• In small groups, craft an argument for the character in *American Born Chinese* who you feel now knows his true self. What might you learn about yourself from studying these three characters?
	For Homework: Read *American Born Chinese* (pp. 199–235) and *Persepolis* (pp. 258–266)
Thursday	Character Analysis Journal Entry
	Image Analysis Journal Entry
	Class Discussion and Activity Topics:
	• Now that we've finished *American Born Chinese*, reflect on how these interrelated stories have influenced your own development.
	• Group Discussion: What factors have influenced Marjane's development? In what ways are those similar/different to Jin, Danny, the Monkey King, and yourselves?
	• Quick write about the roles of context and outside influences on one's self-perception (note that you can draw from Marjane's story)
	For Homework: Read *Persepolis* (pp. 299–311)

(Continued)

Table 7.3 Week 3 (*Continued*)

Friday	Character Analysis Journal Entry
	Image Analysis Journal Entry
	Class Discussion and Activity Topics:
	• In pairs: craft an argument for how Marjane now perceives herself. Be sure and draw evidence from the text
	• Individually: craft an argument for how you now perceive yourself. Again, make sure you reference our texts
	For Homework: Read *Persepolis* (pp. 328–341)
	Begin timeline of character's life and self-perception development (using journals)
	Return to Self-Portrait

Table 7.4 Week 4

Monday	Continue working on timeline of character's life and self-perception development (using journals)
	Return to Personal Mission Statement
	Introduce Graphic Narrative of Self-Perception
Tuesday	Work on Graphic Narratives
	• Analyze models and mentor texts
	• Pre-writing
Wednesday	Work on Graphic Narratives
	• Continue analyzing models and mentor texts
	• Revisit pre-writing
	• Time to compose
Thursday	Work on Graphic Narratives
	• Continue analyzing models and mentor texts
	• Peer review pre-writing, ideas, and work
	• Time to compose
Friday	Work on Graphic Narratives
	• Individual conferences with teacher on graphic narrative plans
	• Continue composing

Table 7.5 Week 5

Monday	Work on Graphic Narratives
	• Structured writers workshop
	• Continue composing
Tuesday	Work on Graphic Narratives
	• Structured writers workshop
	• Continue composing
Wednesday	Work on Graphic Narratives
	• Continue composing
Thursday	Present Graphic Narratives
	For homework: Begin composing Letter to Self
Friday	Present Graphic Narratives
	Time to continue composing Letter to Self
	For homework: Complete Letter to Self

FOSTERING THEMATIC ANALYSIS OF SELF-PERSPECTIVE: SAMPLE ACTIVITIES FOR ELA CLASSROOMS

In the following section, a variety of assignments and activities are described. Teachers can draw from these as they design their own units around self-perception. Classroom teachers know best their students and contexts and are thus most qualified to design instruction around this or any unit. The hope is that teachers find useful examples and models in this chapter and can use them as jumping-off points for their own teaching. The activities described below are also noted in the calendar plan in the previous section. Similar to the other instructional chapters in this book, the discussion of each activity below includes a brief overview and a connection to the anchor text and the instructional unit.

Introductory Activities

Self-Portrait

As an introduction to the unit, and before students begin reading and discussing the texts, it can be helpful to ask students to take some time and develop a self-portrait. To complete this assignment, students can choose any visual composition method they wish. Some, for example, may want to draw or paint a self-portrait, while others may choose a collage. Others still may use photography or any number of other ways to visually represent themselves.

Students may need to be reminded that artistic ability is not important and that it is much more important they make thoughtful and intentional decisions about how to best represent themselves for others to see. The goal of this assignment is less about art and more about asking students to stop and consider how they view themselves and how they believe others view them. Additionally, because the anchor text is a graphic novel, where characters are literally represented visually, this invites students to begin thinking about visual representation.

Personal Mission Statement

A second possible pre-reading assignment for students is to craft a personal mission statement. Such an assignment is ultimately another space for students to reflect and to think about who they are. The statement could be any length, could be formal or informal, and could be designed to respond to any number of specific prompts. Regardless of these decisions, the goal is to task students with using writing to articulate important pieces of themselves.

Sample prompts include:

- What is your purpose in life?
- What are your values and what do you stand for?
- What accomplishments are you working toward?
- What are you and who do you want to be?

In addition to serving as a pre-assessment for teachers and early self-assessment for students, it is important to hang onto these statements (and to their self-portraits) to allow students to return to them toward the end of the unit, after they have read *American Born Chinese* and all the unit texts and engaged in ongoing discussion and reflection on self-perception.

Reading and Discussing the Novel

Character Analysis Journal

One type of journal students can keep throughout the unit, as they read and discuss class texts and as they begin to make connections to themselves and their own lives, is the character analysis journal. The purpose of the character analysis journal is simple—for students to make a note of textual evidence of individual character's decisions, re/actions, and thoughts that contribute to their development of self-perception and for students to record personal connections. Teachers may allow their students a choice: they may select a character from *American Born Chinese* or keep a journal on the development of Marjane in *Persepolis*.

Teachers may choose to ask students to keep one entry per day, per class period, per assigned reading, or per week. This ongoing assignment could, of course, serve as the foundation for a character analysis essay or some other academic piece of writing, but for the purposes of this unit, students' entries are intended to create required moments of textual connection, personal reflection, and individual development. As such, students can use this assignment for the purposes of self-assessment, and they can return to it later in the unit as they plan for and compose their graphic narrative and letter to self.

Timeline of a Character's Life and Self-Perception Development

In conjunction with the character analysis journal, students can compose a timeline of an individual character's life (or multiple characters' lives) and development of self-perception. The timeline serves as a visual representation of the day-to-day work students do in their journal entries and provides them yet another way to make visual composition part of their learning and growth processes. There are many questions students can answer through and as a result of this assignment, but two larger, and critical to the unit's goals, questions are:

- How does the character develop, with regard to self-perception?
- What contributes to and hinders that development?

Combining the character analysis journal and the timeline, students must also consider the question: How do these experiences help you to think more about yourself and your own development? Responding to this question will connect literary characters' experiences with the students' personal self-explorations.

Image Analysis Journal

A second version of a journal teachers can ask students to keep is the image analysis journal. This is specifically relevant to the study of graphic novels and image-driven texts, where images play major roles in how information is created, disseminated, and taken up. While reading *American Born Chinese*, or any other text containing images, students can select one panel or image per day/reading for analysis.

As part of each analytical entry, students will discuss how the selected image or panel represents the character's self-perception and how they know (i.e., what evidence exists and what inferences are they making?) and their own perception of that character. This activity also requires students to consider each of these entries against themselves, what they believe others see and what inferences they might make, and how that impacts their own self-perception.

Students can return to the image analysis journal as they plan for their graphic narratives and as they revisit their self-portraits. In other words, the image analysis journal houses personal references to mentor texts, inner thoughts, and representations of growth manifest across the unit.

Enrichment Activities

Letter to Self

One of the culminating activities for the unit on self-perception is a Letter to Self. The goal of this assignment is to provide students with space and reason to draw on all they have read, analyzed, and talked and written about throughout the unit to meaningfully reflect on themselves, who they are, and how they've grown. This assignment pairs well with the graphic narrative because where the graphic narrative asks students to articulate how they have come to more accurately perceive themselves as a result of the unit, the Letter to Self requires them to compose an intimate and personal explanation for themselves. In other words, the Letter to Self requires a level of vulnerability and honesty vital to students growing as individuals.

In preparing to compose their own Letter to Self, students should return to their character and image analysis journals, their text annotations, and their own memories of unit experiences to begin planning their letter. To guide students through this process, teachers may provide prompting questions, such as: What are you proud of? What have you done/accomplished? Who have you helped, and who has helped you? What have you learned about yourself? And what do you appreciate about yourself? Regardless of length, formality, and so on of the letter itself, the objective should be to scaffold students in pointing out the value, expertise, beauty, and other traits they see in themselves.

Return to Self-Portrait and/or Mission Statement

At the end of the unit, after students have read *American Born Chinese* and the other unit texts, after they have engaged in ongoing analysis, discussion, reflection, and personal connection, they can return to two assignments they completed in the first week of the unit—the self-portrait and personal mission statement. The goal is for students to use this as an opportunity to self-assess their own learning, development, and personal perceptions of self.

Teachers may or may not require students to rework these assignments, but asking them to reflect in some way on how they have grown and what changes they would make and why it can be very beneficial. This process could also be tied to the Letter to Self assignment, where students revisit their early unit work as part of their pre-composing processes.

Graphic Narrative of Self-Perception

One culminating assignment that asks students to use their experiences consuming, analyzing, discussing, and reflecting on two graphic novels is the Graphic Narrative of Self-Perception project. The goal for students is twofold. First, this assignment allows them to demonstrate their skills in rhetorically analyzing and composing a multimodal text—a graphic novel in this case.

Simultaneously learning from and using *American Born Chinese* and *Persepolis* as mentor texts, students utilize the same rhetorical strategies Yang and Satrapi use in creating their own stories. In short, this demonstrates students' critical thinking, their abilities to compose using multiple modes of communication, and their own development of self-perception.

Second, the graphic narrative assignment provides a unique way for students to think through, articulate, and share their own paths to self-perception throughout the unit. Rather than only writing about characters and themselves, they are tasked here with applying what they have learned to make that learning, and their development, visible for others.

There is no shortage of ways to structure this assignment. For example, teachers may require more or less lengthy narratives. For the purposes of this example, students would be asked to compose a front and back cover for their narrative (cover art plays important parts in conveying the meaning of comics and graphic novels) and four to six pages of graphic text (although they should feel free to go beyond) with one to six panels, depending on purpose, on each page.

While artistic ability should play no bearing in assignment criteria, and students should be encouraged to compose their own graphic narrative using whatever artistic mode they feel best fits their rhetorical situation—they may draw, paint, collage, and so on (see, e.g., Cook & Sams, 2018)—they do often feel concerned about how their art will be perceived by others and how it might impact their grades. For those students, there are a number of online and digital tools for creating graphic novels (see Cook & Kirchoff, 2015, 2017; Kirchoff & Cook, 2015).

UNIT MATERIALS INVENTORY

Anchor Text

Yang, G. L. (2006). *American Born Chinese*. New York, NY: First Second Books.

Fiction (will be excerpted)

Cisneros, S. (1991). *The House on Mango Street*. New York, NY: Vintage.

Poetry

"Identity" by Julio Noboa Polanco

Nonfiction

Satrapi, M. (2003). *The complete persepolis*. New York, NY: Pantheon.

Videos

"The Power of Self-Perception" (TED Talk) by Arlando Mba Retrieved April 23, 2020, https://www.youtube.com/watch?v=2PkIlzHwfSA

"The Psychology of Your Future Self" (TED Talk) by Dan Gilbert Retrieved April 23, 2020, https://www.ted.com/talks/dan_gilbert_the_psychology_of_your_future_self?language=en

ADDITIONAL RESOURCES FOR TEACHERS

The materials included in the example unit described above include the unit anchor text, Yang's *American Born Chinese*, a supplemental text, Satrapi's graphic novel *Persepolis*, and a variety of resources and materials (e.g., poetry, videos) meant to engage students in a meaningful study of self-perception. Again, this unit is one example, and teachers are encouraged to design similar or different units drawing from this or other anchor texts. Other possible anchor and unit texts are listed in Table 7.6.

Table 7.6 Additional Resources for Teachers

Fiction
Anderson, L.H. (1999). *Speak*. Farrar, Straus and Giroux.
Anderson, L.H. (2009). *Wintergirls*. Viking.
Beaumont, K. (2004). *I Like Myself!* Harcourt.
Konigsberg, B. (2013). *Openly Straight*. Scholastic.
Murdock, C.G. (2006). *Dairy Queen*. Houghton Mifflin Harcourt.
Palacio, R. J. (2012). *Wonder*. Alfred A. Knopf.
Rowell, R. (2013). *Eleanor & Park*. St. Martin's Griffin.
Stead, R. (2015) *Goodbye Stranger*. Yearling.
Wang, J. (2018). *The Prince and the Dressmaker*. First Second.
Nonfiction
Anderson, L.H. (2019). *Shout*. Penguin Books.
Lewis, J., Aydin, A., & Powell, N. (2013). *March* (Books 1–3). Top Shelf Productions.
Pippins, A. (2016). *Becoming Me: A Work in Progress: Color, Journal & Brainstorm Your Way to a Creative Life*. Random House.
Satrapi, M. (2003). *The Complete Persepolis*. Pantheon.
Skeen, M. & Skeen, K. (2018). *Just as You Are: A Teen's Guide to Self-Acceptance & Lasting Self-Esteem*. Instant Help Books.
Media and Web Resources
Alvord, M. (2017, Sept. 9). For teens knee-deep in negativity, reframing thoughts can help. NPR. Retrieved April 27, 2020, https://www.npr.org/sections/health-shots/201 7/09/09/549133027/ for-teens-knee-deep-in-negativity-reframing-thoughts-can-help
Fraga, J. (2018, Jan. 13). Helping strangers may help teens' self-esteem. NPR. Retrieved April 27, 2020, https://www.npr.org/sections/health-shots/2018/01/13/57 7463475/helping-strangers-may-help-teens-self-esteem
Weinstein, L. (2018, April). *Don't Believe Everything You Think*. TED: Ideas Worth Spreading. Retrieved April 27, 2020, https://www.ted.com/talks/lauren_weinstein _don_t_believe_everything_you_think?language=en

KEY ELEMENTS OF THE INSTRUCTIONAL UNIT

The purpose of this chapter is to share an overview of one example teaching unit designed to foster analysis and reflection on self-perception. This chapter includes the following:

- a unit rationale;
- an overview of essential questions, objectives, and assignments that frame the unit;
- a five-week example unit or unit at a glance, including reading and assignment breakdowns, sequencing of learning, and brief overviews of each week;
- a list of possible before-, during-, and after-reading assignments designed specifically for this unit on self-perception;
- a list of unit texts; and
- additional resources and materials to foster exploration of the unit theme.

Readers may use this example unit, in whole or in part, as part of their own instructional design process.

Bibliography

Anderson, L. H. (1999). *Speak*. Penguin Group.
Anderson, L. H. (2002). *Catalyst*. Viking Press.
Anderson, L. H. (2009). *Wintergirls*. Viking Press.
Anderson, L. H. (2019). *Shout*. Viking Press.
Aronson, M. (2001). *Exploring the myth: The truth about teenagers and reading*. Scarecrow Press.
Aronson, M. (2002). Coming of age. *Publishers Weekly, 249*(6), 82–86.
Austen, J. (1995). *Pride and prejudice*. Modern Library.
Bean, T. W., & Moni, K. (2003). Developing students' critical literacy: Exploring identity construction in young adult fiction. *Journal of Adolescent & Adult Literacy, 46*(8), 638–648.
Bean, T. W., & Rigoni, N. (2001). Exploring the intergenerational dialogue journal discussion of a multicultural young adult novel. *Reading Research Quarterly, 36*(3), 232–248.
Bell, C. (2014). *El Deafo*. Abrams Books.
Benway, R. (2017). *Far from the tree*. HarperTeen, an imprint of HarperCollins Publishers.
Bolton, G. (2014). *Reflective practice: Writing and professional development*. Sage.
Borsheim-Black, C., & Sarigianides, S. T. (2019). *Letting go of literary whiteness: Antiracist literature instruction for White students*. Teachers College Press.
Brown, J. (2009). *Hate list*. Little, Brown and Company.
Brown, J. E., & Stephens, E. C. (1995). *Teaching young adult literature: Sharing the connections*. Wadsworth Publishing.
Bucher, K., & Hinton, K. (2010). *Young adult literature: Exploration, evaluation, and appreciation* (2nd ed.). Allyn & Bacon
Bushman, J. H., & Bushman, K. P. (1997). *Using young adult literature in the English classroom*. Prentice-Hall, Inc.
Cameron, P. (2007). *Someday this pain will be useful to you*. Farrar, Straus and Giroux.

Campbell, J. (2008). *The hero with a thousand faces* (3rd ed.). World Library.
Campbell, P. (2004). The sand in the oyster: YA biblio-bullish trends. *The Horn Book, 80*(1), 61–65.
Cart, M. (2001). The evolution of young adult literature. *Voices from the Middle, 9*(2), 95–97.
Cart, M. (2008). The value of young adult literature. Retrieved May 2, 2020, from http://www.ala.org/yalsa/guidelines/whitepapers/yalit.
Cart, M. (2010). A new literature for a new millennium? The first decade of the Printz awards. *Young Adult Library Services, 8*(3), 28–31.
Cook, M., & Kirchoff, J. S. J. (2015). Graphic novels in the classroom: Suggestions for appropriate multimodal writing projects in graphic novel units. *Minnesota English Journal*. Retrieved March 19, 2020, from http://minnesotaenglishjournal online.org.
Cook, M. P., & Kirchoff, J. S. J. (2017). Teaching multimodal literacy through reading and writing graphic novels. *Language & Literacy, 19*(4), 76–95.
Cook, M. P., & Sams, B. L. (2018). Participating in literacy and the outside world: Consuming, composing, and sharing graphic narratives. In J. S. Dail, S. Witte, & S. T. Bickmore (Eds.), *Young adult literature and the digital world* (pp. 61–78). Rowman & Littlefield.
Cramer, A. (December 21, 2016). Too much of a good thing: A condensed version of the world of Shakespeare. *Dr. Bickmore's YA Wednesday*. Retrieved February 11, 2020, from http://www.yawednesday.com/blog/too-much-of-a-good-thing-a-c ondensed-version-of-the-world-of-shakespeare.
Culham, R. (2018). Rethinking revision: The real work of writing. *Middle Web: All about the Middle Grades*, Wordpress.org. Retrieved January 27, 2020, from www. middleweb.com/37682/rethinking-revision-the-real-work-of-writing/.
de la Peña, M. (2008). *Mexican whiteboy*. Ember.
Dickens, C., Law, G., & Pinnington, A. J. (1998). *Great expectations*. Broadview Press.
Donelson, K. L., & Nilsen, A. P. (1997). *Literature for today's young adults* (5th ed.). Longman.
Ellis, D. (2012). *My name is Parvana*. Groundwood Books.
Fitzgerald, F. S. (1925, 2004). *The great Gatsby*. Scribner.
Flake, S. G. (1999). *The skin I'm in*. Disney. Jump at the Sun.
Glaus, M. (2014). Text complexity and young adult literature: Establishing its place. *Journal of Adolescent & Adult Literacy, 57*(5), 407–416.
Hamby, Z. (2018). Heroes and the hero's journey. Retrieved February 7, 2020, from www.creativeenglishteacher.com.
Hamilton, E. (1969). *Mythology: Timeless tales of gods and heroes*. Little, Brown and Company.
Hayn, J. A., & Bach, B. (2011). This issue. *Theory Into Practice, 50*(3), 173–175.
Heaney, S. (2000). *Beowulf: A new verse translation*. Norton & Company.
Herz, S., & Gallo, D. (1996). *From Hinton to Hamlet: Building bridges between young adult literature and the classics* (1st ed.). Greenwood Press.

Herz, S., & Gallo, D. (2005). *From Hinton to Hamlet: Building bridges between young adult literature and the classics* (2nd ed.). Greenwood Press.
Hiatt, W. (2019). *The problems of teaching Greek mythology.* Bill Hyatt's Author Website. Retrieved February 7, 2020, from https://www.billhiatt.com/2019/05/09/the-problems-of-teaching-greek-mythology/.
Hillocks, G. (2011). *Teaching Argument Writing, grades 6–12.* Heinemann.
Hinton, S. E. (1967). *The outsiders.* Penguin Group.
Homer. (1919, translated). *The Odyssey.* G.P. Putnam's Sons.
Kaplan, J. S., & Olan, E. L. (2017). Young adult literature and today's reader. The many faces, changes, and challenges for teachers and Researchers in the twenty-first century. In J. A. Hayn, J. S. Kaplan, & K. R. Clemmons (Eds.), *Teaching young adult literature today: Insights, considerations, and perspectives for the classroom teacher* (2nd ed., pp. 9–26). Rowman & Littlefield.
Kaywell, J. F. (2001). Conversations from the commissions: Preparing teachers to teach young adult literature. *English Education, 33*(4), 323–327. Retrieved May 3, 2020, from http://www.ncte.org/library/NCTEFiles/Resources/Journals/EE/0334-july01/EE0334Conversations.pdf.
Keplinger, K. (2018). *That's not what happened.* Scholastic Press.
Khorram, A. (2018). *Darius the great is not okay.* Penguin Random House.
Kirchoff, J. S. J., & Cook, M. (2015). Overviewing software applications for graphic novel creation in the post-secondary and secondary classroom. *SANE: Sequential Art Narrative in Education, 2*(1). Retrieved April 11, 2020, from http://digitalcommons.unl.edu/sane/vol2/iss1/1.
Lai, T. (2011). *Inside out and back again.* HarperCollins.
Lee, H. (1960, 2014). *To kill a mockingbird.* HarperCollins.
Lipsyte, R. M. (1967). *The contender.* HarperCollins.
Manning, M. L., & Bucher, K. T. (2009). *Teaching in the middle school.* Allyn & Bacon.
McCormick, P. (2006). *Sold.* Hyperion Books for Children.
Merriam-Webster's encyclopedia of literature. (1995). Merriam-Webster.
Oates, J. C. (2003). *Freaky green eyes.* HarperCollins.
Pitre, L. (2020). Choosing love over hate: Raising students who understand bullying and its dangerous consequences with *Hate List* by Jennifer Brown. In V. Malo-Juvera & P. Greathouse (Eds.), *Breaking the taboo with young adult literature.* Rowman & Littlefield.
Pitre, L., & Bickmore, S. (2018). Discussing war and death in *A Separate Peace* by John Knowles. In S. Bickmore & M. Falter (Eds.), *Moving beyond personal loss to societal grieving: Discussing death's societal impact through literature in the secondary ELA classroom.* Rowman & Littlefield.
Reynolds, J. (2017). *Ghost.* Atheneum/A Catlyn Dlouhy Book
Reynolds, J., & Kiely, B. (2015). *All American boys.* Simon & Schuster.
Roberts, M. (2013). Teaching young adult literature: YA literature belongs in the classroom because. *English Journal, 102*(5), 89–90.
Romano, T. (1987). *Clearing the way: Working with teenage writers.* Heinemann Educational Books, Inc.

Salvner, G. M. (2001). Lessons and lives: Why young adult literature matters. *The ALAN Review, 28*(3), 9.

Satrapi, M. (2003). *The complete Persepolis*. Pantheon.

Shakespeare, W. (1998). *Hamlet*. Signet Classic.

Smith, M., & Wilhelm, J. (2010). *Fresh takes on teaching literary elements: How to teach what really matters about character, setting, point of view, and theme*. Scholastic.

Stallworth, B. J. (2006). The relevance of young adult literature. *Educational Leadership, 63*(7), 59–63.

Stevenson, N. (2015). *Nimona*. HarperCollins.

Stone, N. (2017). *Dear Martin*. Penguin Random House.

Telgemeier, R. (2010). *Smile*. Scholastic.

Thein, A. H., Guise, M., & Sloan, D. L. (2011). Problematizing literature circles as forums for discussion of multicultural and political texts. *Journal of Adolescent & Adult Literacy, 55*(1), 15–24.

Thomas, A. (2017). *The hate u give*. HarperCollins.

Violatti, C. (2019, April). *Zarathustra: The rise of Zoroastrianism in Ancient Persia*. Brewminate: A bold blend of news and ideas. Retrieved March 5, 2020, from https ://brewminate.com/zarathustra-the-rise-of-zoroastrianism-in-ancient-persia/.

We Need Diverse Books. (2020, April 30). Retrieved May 27, 2020, from https:// diversebooks.org/.

Woodson, J. (2014). *Brown girl dreaming*. Penguin Group.

Yang, G. L. (2006). *American born Chinese*. First Second Books.

Index

abolitionist movements, 26
abuse, 29
academic skills: building, 33; enhancing, 21
academic standards, 32
accountability, 5
activities: for analysis of good *versus* bad, right *versus* wrong concept, 71–79; enrichment, 44–47; for self-discovery in classrooms, 38–47; for self-perception conceptual teaching unit, 103–7; for sensory details, 46–47
adolescence: defining, 5–6; development during, 83
adolescent activism, 58
adolescents, 2; characters viewed by, 31; critical reading and, 7–8; interaction of, 86; marketing to, 9; pressure on, 29; reading and, 7; social issues relevant to, 10; teaching, 6–7; voice of, 64
adulthood, 5
agency, 5
All American Boys (Reynolds and Kiely), 3, 57–61, 64–66, 79
American Born Chinese (Yang), 3, 87–96
American Dream, 1

anger, 23, 32
anti-heroes, 20
anti-racism, 3, 26
argumentative essay, 78–79
argumentative writing skills, 3, 71
assessments: post-, 36, 65, 78–79; pre- 33, 34, 38, 67–68, 103–4; self-, 38–39, 95, 104, 106
authors, lessons and messages for readers, 14

behavior, 5, 46
Blume, Judy, 10
book awards, 79
bravery, 18, 60
bullying, 10, 23, 29, 40

calendar: flexibility of, 33; for good *versus* bad, right *versus* wrong conceptual teaching unit, 68–70; for self-discovery conceptual teaching unit, 33–37; for self-perception conceptual teaching unit, 97–102
Campbell, Joseph, 17–18, 23
Cart, Michael, 9–10
censorship, 79
change, success, transformation and, 20
character analysis journal, 104
Character Identity Web, 35, 41–42

115

Character Mind Map, 65, 70, 73, 74
characters: adolescents view of, 31; analyzing, 34; reactions, decisions and consequences for, 15; stories of, 91; teenagers as, 11, 23, 24, 30, 57–58, 89
childhood, 5; lack of, 29; leaving, 14
"Choices," 68, 71–72
choices, making, 84
Chopin, Kate, 9, 35
civil rights movement, 61
classrooms: activities for self-discovery in, 38–47; diversity in, 2, 6, 29; as safe space, 6–7
cognition, 5
collaboration, 7
communication modes, 2, 106
communities, 10, 42
community identity project, 42–44
community members, 42–43
conceptual teaching unit: on good *versus* bad, right *versus* wrong concept, 67–72; self-discovery focused, 29–37; on self-perception, 94–107; unit materials inventory, 48–50, 79–81, 107–9
confidence, 64
conflicts, 11
The Contender (Lipsyte), 10
Cormier, Robert, 10
Cornell Notes, 34–35
Critical Literature Circles, 8
Critical Race Theory, 86
critical reading, adolescents and, 7–8
critical thinking: about communities, 42; sample questions for inspiring, 66–67, 79; writing, personal development and, 30
cruelty, 10
cultural backgrounds, 4
cultural diversity, 11
cultures, 2, 42
curriculums: materials, students and, 21; reading, 1

Daly, Maureen, 9–10
Departure Act, 18, 21
dialogue journals, 65, 70, 73
dignity, 18
displacement, 40
diversity: in classrooms, 2, 6, 29; cultural, 11; gender, 11, 19; social, 11
Duncan, Lois, 10

ego, 90
emotions, 5
Endless Search, 39
engagement: with literature, 95–96; motivation and, 7
environmental issues, 11
equality, 26, 66, 74
equity, 26, 74
ethnic backgrounds, 4
ethnicity, 41–42, 84

fairy tales, 3, 14, 52–54
family, 30; ethnicity and, 41–42; love from, 25
feedback, effective and constructive, 36
folktales, 20
foster care, 40
freedom, structured, 7
friendship, 12, 24, 39–40, 42; and hard choices, 51

gender, 20, 23, 84
gender diversity, 11, 19
generalization, 6
global politics, 11
good *versus* bad, right *versus* wrong concept, 51–52, 61; activities for analysis of, 71–79; conceptual teaching unit on, 67–72; in fairy tales and mythology, 52–54; learning, 63
Graffiti Activity, 65, 70, 75, *76*
graphic narrative assignment, 95, 106–7
Grisham, John, 9

heartbreak, 2

heritage, 25, 90
heroes: archetypal, 20, 31; concept of, 17; defining, 19
hero narrative, 19–20
hero's journey, 2–3, 17–18; as life changing, 23; as self-discovery journey, 26–27; teaching, 21–23
Hinton, S. E., 10
history, cultures, identity and, 42
homelessness, 6, 29
Homer, 17–19
honesty, 18
human behavior, 14
human relationships, 1
human rights, 26

identity: cultures, history and, 42; development of, 3, 29; knowledge of, 31; racial, ethnic, 26; self-discovery, self-acceptance and, 31; understanding, 38–39
identity crisis, 2
identity map, 43
identity struggles, 23, 91; factors contributing to, 24; societal definitions and, 26
image analysis journal, 105
impulse, temptation, anger and, 32
independence: defining adolescent, 5; working with students' varying levels of, 7, 29, 46, 78
information sources, multimodality of, 10
Initiation Act, 18, 21
insecurities, 84
insight, patience, perseverance and, 32
instructional design, 8
integrity, 66

jealousy, 90
journal prompts, 39–40
journal writing, 34, 36; benefit of, 95; reflective, 39–40

Kiely, Brendan, 3, 57–61, 64–66, 79

kindness, 18
King, Stephen, 9
knowledge: background, 30; of identity, 31; literary experiences, teenagers and, 20–24; of writing process, 36

language, as accessible, 11
Lee, Harper, 85–87, 92
legends, 3, 18, 20
lesson plans, 33
Letter to Self, 105–6
LGBTQ, 4, 19, 87
Lion King, 13–14
Lipsyte, Robert, 10
listening skills, 12
literary analysis, 7–8, 66
literary experiences, 20–24
literature, 1; as ally, 7; engaging with, 95–96; personal connection with, 8; as vehicle for self-reflection, 93
Lopez, Alonzo, 39
The Lord of the Rings, 22
loss, 12; of loved ones, 6; of parents, 29
love: Aphrodite and representations of, 54; familial, 25; universal themes of, 12

main idea, 13–14
marketing, to adolescents, 9
maturation, 30
mental health issues, 10
Mexican Whiteboy (Peña), 3, 30, 34, 89; overview of, 23–24; passages from, 44, *45*, 46; reading and discussion of, 38; self-discovery, thematic exploration and, 24–27
modeling, 7
monomyth structure, 18. *See also* hero's journey
motion pictures, 22
motivation, engagement and, 7
mythology, 3, 18, 20, 52–54

narration, voice and, 11

narrative techniques: analyzing, 44–46; examples of, *45*
narrative tools, 11
narrative writing, 35. *See also* personal narrative writing
nonfiction, 31

The Odyssey (Homer), 17–19
Ordinary World, 18
The Outsiders (Hinton), 10

patience, perseverance, insight and, 32
peer interaction, 7
Peña, Matt de la, 3, 23–27, 30, 34, 38, 44–46, 89
Persepolis (Satrapi), 3–4, 94–95
perseverance, patience, insight and, 32
personal development: critical thinking, writing and, 30; growth and, 7
personal mission statement, 103–4
personal narrative writing, 31, 36, 40, 42, 47
poetry, 31
poetry gallery walk, 72
police brutality, racism and, 58–61
poverty, 6, 29
privilege, 26

race, 20, 25
racial discrimination, 26
racial struggles, 26
racism, 12; challenging, 64; police brutality and, 58–61
RAFTE strategy (role, audience, format, topic, expectations), 78–79
reading, 12; adolescents and, 7; critical, 7–8; for pleasure, 30
relationship building, 7
relevance, 7
responsibility, 65–66
Return Act, 18, 21
Reynolds, Jason, 3, 57–61, 64–66, 79

Salvner, Gary, 11–12
Satrapi, Marjane, 3–4, 94–95
Say Something strategy, 34, 40, *41*
scaffolding, 7; building, 30; examples of, 46
Second Chance writing activity, 65, 71, 76–78
self-acceptance, 3, 12, 31, 83–84, 91
self-assessment, 6, 39
self-confidence, 83–84
self-construction, 3, 12; exploring, 23; process of, 30
self-discovery, 2, 20–21, 84, 92; activities for, in classrooms, 38–47; as complicated, 24; conceptual teaching unit focused on, 29–30; exploring, 23, 34–36; hero's journey as journey to, 26–27; identity, self-acceptance and, 31; personal narrative writing of, 42; questions guiding journey to, 32; thematic analysis of, 38–47; thematic exploration, *Mexican Whiteboy* and, 24–26
self-evaluation mechanism, 84
self-exploration, relevant process of, 21
selflessness, 18
self-perception, 3, 83–84; conceptual teaching unit on, 94–107; literary study of, 87–92; as relevant literary theme, 85–86; shifting, 93
self-portrait activity, 103
self-reflection, 87, 93
self-reliance, 83
self-worth, 12, 90
Senses Poem, 46
sensory details, activity for, 46–47
sentence starters, for *Say Something* strategy, 40, *41*
setting, analyzing, 34
Seventeenth Summer (Daly), 9–10
sexuality, 20, 23
Shakespeare, William: tragedies by, 52, 54–57; works by, 1
short stories, 3, 14; building skills using, 30
slavery, 53

small-group work, 40–41
social classes, 10
social diversity, 11
social injustice, 10, 60
social issues, relevant to adolescents, 10
social justice, 58, 66
social norms, 85
socioeconomic backgrounds, 4
Socratic seminar, 65, 71
success, transformation, change and, 20
superheroes, study of, 22
support groups, 25–26

teachers: instructional strategies of, 33; questions used by, 14–15, 66; reflective questions for, 21; safe space created by, 6–7; support provided by, 51
technology, advances in, 10
TED Talks, 36
teenagers: experience of, 17; knowledge, literary experiences and, 20–24
temptation, anger, impulse and, 32
text selection, 8, 12; questions to guide, 87
textual evidence, 14–15
thematic analysis, of self-discovery, 38–47
thematic exploration: self-discovery, *Mexican Whiteboy* and, 24–27; YAL and, 58–61
thematic investigations, 2–3
theme, 13–15
timeline, of character life and self-perception development, 104–5
To Kill a Mockingbird (Lee), 85–87, 92
tolerance, 85
topic, 13–14
transformation, success, change and, 20
trauma, 58

unit materials inventory: for good *versus* bad, right *versus* wrong concept, 79–81; for self-discovery conceptual teaching unit, 48–50; for self-perception conceptual teaching unit, 107–9
universal literary themes, the importance of utilizing, 2, 5–6, 12

values, exploring and refining adolescent students', 23, 32, 39, 57, 63, 104
value systems, 31
visual context, 91
voice: of adolescents, 64; narration and, 11
vulnerability, 17, 106

We Need Diverse Books organization, 10
whiteness, 24, 25, 58
Whiteness Studies, First and Second Wave, 86
writing, 12; critical thinking, personal development and, 30; narrative writing, 35; personal narrative, 31, 36, 40, 42, 47. *See also* journal writing
writing process, 31, 36
writing skills, 32; improving and strengthening, 40, 47, 64

YAL. *See* Young Adult Literature (YAL)
Yang, Gene Luen, 3, 87–96
Young Adult Library Services Association, 10
Young Adult Literature (YAL), 2, 7; adolescent experiences in, 23; books discussing, 13; characteristics of, 8–10; as complex and rigorous, 10–11; criteria for, 11; publishers, 13; thematic exploration and, 58–61

Zoroaster (Zarathustra), 52

About the Authors

Leilya A. Pitre is assistant professor of English Education with secondary school and college teaching experience in various public and private settings. She taught English as a foreign language in the Ukraine and ELA/English in public schools in the United States for over twenty years. Currently, she teaches methods courses for preservice teachers, literary analysis, American Literature, and Young Adult literature in the English Department at Southeastern Louisiana University. Her research interests include teacher preparation, field experiences of preservice English teachers, secondary school teaching, and teaching of Young Adult and multicultural literature. Leilya is coeditor of *Study and Scrutiny: Research on Young Adult Literature* and a member of the English Language Arts Teacher Educator (ELATE) committee at NCTE.

Mike P. Cook is associate professor of English Education at Auburn University, where he teaches undergraduate and graduate courses within the English Education program. He taught high school English for several years in North Carolina, where he made YAL central in his work with students. He also worked as an instructional/literacy coach for a N.C. school district before moving on to higher education. His teaching and research interests include YAL, multimodal literacy, and teacher identity development, including the overlaps and connections between them. His scholarship has appeared in *The ALAN Review*, *SIGNAL Journal*, *Journal of Language and Literacy Education*, and *English Teaching: Practice & Critique*, among others.

www.ingramcontent.com/pod-product-compliance
Lightning Source LLC
Chambersburg PA
CBHW020749230426
43665CB00009B/550